t r a p

in

HITLeR'S
HeLL

trapped
in
HITLer's
HeLL

a YOUNG JEWISH GIRL DISCOVERS *the* MESSIAH'S
faITHfULNess *in the* MIDST *of the* HOLOCAUST

aNita DItTMaN

with JaN MarKeLL

WND Books

tRAppeD *in* HitLeR's HeLL

Published by WND Books®, Washington, D.C. WND Books is a registered trademark of
WorldNetDaily.com, Inc. ("WND")

4th Edition, Previously titled *Angels in the Camp*, published by Tyndale House 1979 ISBN
0842300716.

Unless otherwise noted, all Scripture quotations are taken from the King James Version (public
domain). Scripture quotations marked nasb are taken from the NEW AMERICAN STANDARD
BIBLE®, © The Lockman Foundation 1960, 1962, 1963, 1968, 1971, 1972, 1973, 1975, 1977,
1995. Used by permission.

Book designed by Mark Karis.   Cover photo © Tim De Boeck.

WND Books are distributed to the trade by:
Midpoint Trade Books, 27 West 20th Street, Suite 1102, New York, New York 10011
WND Books are available at special discounts for bulk purchases. WND Books, Inc.,
also publishes books in electronic formats. For more information call (541) 474-1776 or visit
www.wndbooks.com.

First Edition   Print ISBN: 978-1-936488-12-4   eBook ISBN: 978-1-936488-13-1

Library of Congress Catalog-in-Publication Data
Dittman, Anita.
[Angels in the camp]
Trapped in Hitler's hell : a young Jewish girl discovers the Messiah's
faithfulness in the midst of the Holocaust / by Anita Dittman with Jan
Markell. -- 4th edition.
    pages cm
"Previously titled Angels in the camp; published by Tyndale House,
1979"--Title page verso.
ISBN 978-1-936488-12-4 (paperback) -- ISBN 978-1-936488-13-1 (ebook)
1. Dittman, Anita--Childhood and youth 2. Jews--Germany--Biography. 3.
Jewish girls--Germany--Biography. 4. Holocaust, Jewish
(1939-1945)--Germany--Personal narratives. 5. Jewish children in the
Holocaust--Germany. 6. Christian converts from Judaism--Biography. 7.
Jesus Christ--Influence. I. Markell, Jan, 1944- II. Title.
DS135.G5D583 2014
940.53'18092--dc23
[B]
                            2013051150

Printed in the United States of America
14 15 16 17 18 19 MP 9 8 7 6 5 4 3 2 1

table of contents

Since my arrival in America in 1946, it has been my dream and prayer to share with others the glorious miracles the Lord performed during my twelve and a half years of persecution under the Nazi regime. However, in the Lord's timing, the book did not take shape until sometime in the winter of 1977, after I had reaffirmed my faith in Jesus Christ and renewed my total commitment to Him during one of Billy Graham's Crusades on TV.

I dedicate this book to the glory of God and with deepest gratitude in memory of my pastor and beloved friend the late Bishop Ernst Hornig of Germany, who through his perfect Christ-like example first led me into a living relationship with my Savior when I was twelve.

My sincere appreciation also goes to my dear friend Dr. H. Allan Talley of Hope Presbyterian Church, Minneapolis, whose care and concern for me have been a constant source of comfort and encouragement. He in turn introduced me to the talented young writer of this book, Jan Markell. Her friendship and her spiritual depth have had a powerful impact upon my life. May the testimonies on these pages awaken each reader to the full realization that Christ is alive today and that His miracles, love, and forgiveness are unlimited.

Anita Dittman

this book is dedicated to my parents, Ben and Helga Markell. My father's Jewish heritage gave me a passion to understand the truth of all things Jewish, including the Holocaust. He died a believer in 2001. My mother prayed me through many serious circumstances in life, including major illness. She was a Proverbs 31 woman who never gave up hope that her husband would become a believer and I would recover from these illnesses and serve the kingdom of God in full-time ministry. She died of cancer in 1987, much too soon. I so look forward to our heavenly reunion.

Jan Markell

Be merciful unto me, O God, be merciful unto me: for my soul trusteth in thee: yea, in the shadow of thy wings will I make my refuge until these calamities be overpast.

Psalms 57:1

foreword

I t's a strange and sobering thought to ponder that none of us have any say about when or where we are born. I was delivered from my mother's womb just after the Second World War during a time of peace and prosperity in New Zealand—a country that has never been invaded by an enemy.

How different my life would have been if I had been born in Europe just twenty years earlier.

My Jewish ancestors fled European anti-Semitism back in the late 1800s. Had they chosen to stay and hide in Poland until the persecution passed, my life would have been radically different. When I consider what it would have been like to experience firsthand the horror of the Holocaust, I shudder at the thought. That's why books that tell of Jewish persecution in Nazi Germany are so meaningful to me.

Trapped in Hitler's Hell is more than just a gripping story. It is living history. It's a human experience of the Christian faith that induces empathy from the reader. I was so moved by its account that I sought out Jan Markell to say how its pages had affected me.

May God use this wonderful publication to remind us of the darkest of times in human history, to help us appreciate liberty, and to display the power of Christian faith in times of gross darkness.

Ray Comfort, author of Hitler, God, and the Bible and producer of the film 180.

pROLoGue

L ike Ray Comfort, my Jewish ancestors fled a persecuted
land more than a hundred years ago. The pogroms of
Russia before the Russian Revolution were a mini-holocaust.
Author Joel Rosenberg and I joke that our grandparents may have
been under the hay of the same fleeing wagon, praying no Russian
pitchfork would strike one of the kids.

Thankfully, my Lithuanian grandparents went straight to Ellis
Island and never made a detour into Europe. They likely would not
have come out alive.

People who do not know persecution don't reflect on such
things, nor do their offspring. But if it is in your family history, you
ponder it often—*you never take freedom for granted.*

About the time this book first came out decades ago, the Iranian
Revolution was heating up. A mystery man by the name of Ayatollah
Ruhollah Khomeini was coming out of the shadows and opposing
the government of Mohammad Reza Pahlavi, the Shah of Iran. U.S.
president Jimmy Carter ignored the Shah's pleas for help, and Carter's weakness emboldened the Iranians who sided with Khomeini.

Back in the late 1970s, I am not sure how many people realized a new war was brewing. That a second "Holocaust" was on
the minds of the mullahs of Iran and the leaders of other Islamic

strongholds. While no one back then could have envisioned air-planes flying into tall buildings and causing them to pancake down, killing nearly three thousand Americans, people should have been aware that new Hitlers were arising in the Islamic world, who would actually deny the Holocaust. The most outspoken in this century was Mahmoud Ahmadinejad of Iran, who was voted out of office in 2013. His successor, Hassan Rouhani, has a softer tone but is still determined to wipe out the very memory of Israel's existence. He is a cunning man who tweeted holiday greetings to the Jews during the fall feasts in 2013, yet wants their demise as much as Ahmadinejad.

The great Old Testament prophet Jeremiah wrote: "'Behold, I am going to send for many fishermen,' declares the LORD, 'and they will fish for them; and afterwards I will send for many hunters, and they will hunt them from every mountain and every hill and from the clefts of the rocks" (Jer. 16:16 NASB). Many of us with a Jewish heritage ponder the meaning of Jeremiah's words. The prophet was writing about the Jews. Could the "fishermen" be the Zionists who pleaded with the Jews to flee Europe in the 1920s and 1930s because the "hunters," the Nazis, would hunt them from every mountain and hill and cleft of the rocks? The Zionists urged all Jews to flee to Palestine, as Israel was called back then. Most Jews scoffed at the idea because Israel wasn't even a nation yet. Besides, they had a hard time believing the carnage would end up being so devastating.

Jews won't make such a mistake again. Today they take seriously the Islamic world's proclamations of their intent to annihilate them, and Israeli planes are always prepared to go on the offense or defense should a modern-day Hitler give the orders to exterminate them.

The question of many, both Jew and non-Jew, is why has the devil wanted the Jews exterminated, really, since the beginning of time? Haman, Pharaoh, and so many others were all too quick to become the instrument that would wipe out the Jews. What, or who, drove them?

Clearly, the devil knows the important role Jews play in our world, and particularly at the very end of time. I believe the enemy is convinced that if he could wipe them out, he could save his own skin, as God's end-time plan of the ages would be foiled. He knows the Bible better than most Christians do, yet he cannot alter the course of events. But he never stops trying. He never stops inspiring people to make the Jewish people an inconvenient memory that is blotted out.

As Dr. Natan P. F. Kellermann notes in his 2009 book *Holocaust Trauma: Psychological Effects and Treatment*:

> There is something unprecedented about the European Holocaust. . . . For the first time in the bloodstained history of the human race, a decision was birthed in a modern state, in the midst of a civilized continent, to track down, register, mark, isolate, dispossess, humiliate, concentrate, transport, and murder every single person of an ethnic group as defined by the perpetrators.

This was targeted at an ethnic group who so generously contributed to the culture of the world; to a people who have borne the brunt of enmity toward them because they dared to be different and dared to insist on their difference.

This resolution was targeted at an ethnic group who have so generously contributed to the world culture, yet have borne the brunt of enmity toward them because they dared to be different and to insist on their difference.

Christianity is very Jewish! Jesus is Jewish. Most writers of the Bible were Jewish. The Bible says in Jeremiah 31 that as long as you see the sun and the moon and the stars as a part of the fixed ordinance, you can be assured that the Jews remain God's called-out people.

That the Jews have survived at all for the last twenty-five hundred years is supernatural. No other nation has or even could endure similar treatment. The Jews' existence is the greatest testimony of a loving God who keeps His covenants to both the Jew and the Christian.

May you ponder these things as you flip through the pages of this book, which chronicles one of the most amazing stories you will ever read.

—Jan Markell, November 2013

1

a new era — "heiL hitLeR!"

"They're here," I gasped as I burst through the door. "The passports and visas are here."

"Oh, thank You, Jesus," Mother exclaimed softly. Even my sister, Hella, showed unusual emotion. Mother tore open the envelope and looked at the enclosed official forms, but her wonderful anticipation diminished as she read them. Her joy turned to a painful realization that only one of us had received a visa and a passport.

"Only Hella's papers are here," Mother sighed. "But they insist that yours and mine will be here by the end of August. At least Hella can go free, Anita. We must rejoice for her and trust God some more for you and me. We can meet Hella in London."

"Mother, Jesus won't let us down," I replied. "Pastor Hornig says we please Him the most when we have faith in Him. See what an opportunity we have to have faith in Jesus, Mother?"

The corners of her mouth smiled weakly as she set Hella's paper aside. "I'm learning to trust Him, Anita."

Since Hella would leave on August 31, we frantically made preparations for her departure. Pastor Hornig gave her some money, surely taking food away from his family's table. We wondered if God was delivering Hella first because her faith was so small that she could not endure any more waiting. A faint signal on our radio from an underground station had told us Hitler was on the move and might invade Poland any day. During the week, we'd been having mock blackouts in Breslau, which according to Mother spelled war. Without a doubt there would be a countdown from freedom for us before the war began. Only our trust in Jesus kept us calm.

* * *

August was slipping away so quickly, with no word yet. Each day's mail brought only disappointment. Thus, the day of Hella's departure produced a mixture of emotions: We were happy for her, but also conscious that our own papers had not arrived. As we bid her farewell, our tears of joy for Hella were mingled with tears of fear and confusion.

"Hella, you must thank Jesus for your freedom," I insisted. "He has worked a miracle for you."

Hella nodded, but her heart had not mellowed toward Christ.

"We will meet you in London soon," Mother said as she embraced Hella, "and our prayers will be with you every day. Pastor Hornig's contact in London can be trusted. You do whatever they say, but don't send any mail to us here in Germany. We'll probably meet you within a month."

The antiquated train gave a sharp whistle. Our good-byes were short, for we were sure we would soon be reunited. Pushing forward to board the train were hundreds of frightened, fleeing people— people thankful for a new lease on life, but riddled with fear for loved ones being left behind—sometimes their whereabouts unknown.

We all embraced one more time, and Hella turned and boarded, waving an enthusiastic good-bye to us. I took Mother's hand as we watched the rest of the crowd board. A few minutes later the train jerked forward; then it chugged away until it was out of sight, but we could see its thick, black smoke dotting the horizon.

The next day Germany invaded Poland. Also on that day the German borders were closed, and Germany thereafter refused all mail from England. Our visas and passports were to come from England; they were in the mail but never made it to us. Two days later, on September 3, 1939, England and France declared war on Germany.

Mother and I were trapped in Hitler's hell.

But the trap had begun to close for us six years earlier, when I was a small child . . .

The dance was beautifully performed by six-year-old Anita Dittman. Her skill and grace at ballet far exceed her years. Nevertheless, we Germans no longer wish to be entertained by a Jew.

Mother read the review to me from a morning paper she had found lying on the street. Her words, though spoken in hushed tones, reverberated throughout the house. They fell on my unbelieving ears and caused an instant flood of tears—tears of a child too young to grasp the meaning of such a word as *anti-Semitism*. All I knew was that my dream of growing up to become the world's best ballet dancer had just been shattered. It didn't matter that we didn't understand why we were being persecuted. Jews, along with communists and other anti-Nazis,* were not allowed to question it. Soon we would have only one freedom: to die.

* * *

I was a first grader in Breslau, Germany, at the time. It was 1933, and the Nazi fires were only kindling sparks. In time, they would erupt into a holocaust in which millions would be consumed by its hate, its lies, and its unfounded prejudices. Already I couldn't

* Short for National Socialist, a political party of Germany.

come home after school without suffering a stoning or a beating. Particularly the little German boys, swollen with Aryan* pride and propaganda that told them to stamp out inferiors, delighted in ganging up on me. And this was just the beginning of what would be a twelve-year nightmare—twelve years of waiting for a knock on the door from the Gestapo; for a loved one to be dragged away by the hair or the beard to points unknown; for a boxcar ride, to be jammed in with hundreds of frightened, weeping people on their way to a death camp; or for a merciful bullet to end it all.

Among those unfortunate Jews, I was to be one of the few with a real home. I would come to know Jesus, who would offer peace in the midst of the turmoil. After all, wasn't He the Prince of Peace?

Hella with a neighbor child and Anita (3 years old), 1930, before the war.

---

* Although the term had no ethnological validity, *Aryan*, whom the Nazis considered to be a member of the superior race, was used by the Nazis to mean "a Caucasian of non-Jewish descent."

My mother, Hilde, was one of thirteen children born into an Orthodox Jewish home in Germany. Since they were a pitifully poor family, they could not afford to send Mother to a Jewish school. Public schools always taught religion, so Mother, along with other poor Jewish children, had to hear about Jesus of Nazareth.

Hella and Anita, 1930

The name of Jesus was an offense to most Jews. Under the banner of the cross, millions of Jews had died throughout history. Yet something within Mother was awakened whenever she read about Jesus in her textbooks. She couldn't deny the tug at her heart as she studied His life, while Judaism left a spiritual vacuum this Man from Galilee beckoned to fill. She did not dare utter her curiosity aloud, yet she found herself saying quietly, "Maybe Jesus is the God I've been looking for."

But at nineteen she, like so many other searching young people, gave in to the lure of a cult: theosophy, which is similar to Hinduism and teaches reincarnation. Christ was placed on the same level as Buddha and Muhammad, and she could worship a multitude of equal gods. She renounced her Judaism and ran from Jesus. Little did she know then that she would one day call upon the name of *Yeshua* ("Jesus") for mercy, protection, deliverance, and, most important of all, salvation.

Father was an Aryan German and a devout atheist. He was

active in Germany's Social Democratic Party, Hitler's archrival, and served as editor of the *Volkswacht*, an anti-Nazi newspaper in the city of Breslau.*

We were comfortably wealthy and rented a row house. Only the very rich could afford to own a house on its own lot.

But the Nazis forced Father's newspaper to close down, putting all the employees out of work. Father was forced to train new Nazi personnel so the paper could crank out propaganda in Breslau and its surrounding province, perhaps Germany's largest stronghold of swastika supporters.

At the same time, they put unbearable pressure on Father to leave Mother, my sister, and me, for the Nazis discouraged any relations between Germans and Jews. Many intermarriages were dissolved or annulled by the state. It was considered a grave abomination to pollute the German race by marrying Jews. Father's only real affection was for my sister, Hella, and he seldom tried to hide his lukewarm feelings for me and Mother. He often reminded me how disappointed he was that I wasn't a son. To protect my desperately hurt feelings, I pulled away from Father and cut him off emotionally. When he left our family, I shed no tears. Perhaps my inner longing for a loving father drove me to my heavenly Father so early in life.

Father left us in 1933 to flee the Nazis, who were hunting all members of the Social Democratic Party. We went on welfare and had to move into a tiny, one-room apartment not far from our town house. But we were grateful, for though our quarters were cramped, the apartment was relatively clean and in a decent section of Breslau. Yet hardships were ever present and growing. We had no money for anything but rent and a meager amount for food—the equivalent of about twenty cents per meal. My precious ballet lessons, which had been my only real escape in Nazi Germany, had to stop. When

---

* This is the German name for what is now Wroclaw, Poland—a city returned to that country after World War II.

I danced, I danced away all cares and fears. I slipped into a make-believe world filled with all the normal delights of a six-year-old and felt totally free and fulfilled. Now that was gone.

Living above us in our apartment complex was a Catholic family who invited me to attend church with them one Sunday. Mother, who recognized the same spiritual hunger within me that she had felt as a child, allowed me to go. I too, was being exposed to Jesus in public school religion classes, which ironically, the God-hating Hitler had not stopped. As I sat through the cathedral service that Sunday morning, God's Spirit began to move in my young life. I gasped in awe at the breathtaking stained-glass windows depicting the life of Jesus. How graphically I saw His birth, life, death, and resurrection. Jesus had to be more than a carpenter masquerading as a king. With all the religious options I had as a six-year-old, it is incredible that I could discern that Jesus truly was God. I did not believe in the rituals of Judaism or Catholicism, or Father's ardent atheism, or Mother's wavering practice of theosophy. The Spirit of God touched a little girl; in a few years I would take up my cross and follow Him. Mother had allowed the sophistries of the intellectual world to lure her away from the God of the Old and New Testaments. Realizing her failure, she gave me freedom to seek the God of my choice.

Perhaps to me Jesus was just a father substitute or the fantasy of a child looking for security and love in a world of hate and fear. I don't know; at the time all that mattered was that I felt safe with Him. I knew He understood me, and I was sure He heard me when I talked to Him. He would become my best Friend even before He became my Lord and Savior.

* * *

Adolf Hitler came to power because the confused and senile President Hindenburg permitted it. In the early 1930s, Germany was in the throes of the economic depression that had begun on

Wall Street in October 1929. The depression's effects had been felt in Germany almost immediately; by 1933 nearly one-third of the country was unemployed.

During the 1930 elections, the Nazis made the most noise because they were violently anticommunist and had the backing of wealthy German industrialists. Scoring giant gains in the Reichstag, Germany's legislative assembly, their representation jumped from 12 to 107.

By 1932, the Nazis had become even stronger as they rallied around the leadership of Adolf Hitler. With his staff, Hitler traveled to every village and hamlet to gain votes, his unemployment bandwagon gaining so much support that the Nazis more than doubled their parliament seats.

Then Hitler was offered the German vice-chancellorship peacefully and legally. He refused. He wanted nothing short of the chancellorship, which would give him power almost equal to Hindenburg's. Later in 1932, he was offered the full chancellorship, with limited conditions. Again he held out, protesting the conditions.

By then Germany's streets were loud with riots and political fights. Brown-shirted Nazis fought all opponents—particularly left-wing ones—openly in the streets as well as in dark alleys.

Finally, in January 1933, Hitler was made the chancellor of a coalition government; Hindenburg, nearly eighty-five and no longer able to read, remained president. A torchlight parade was held on January 30. A new era of history had opened—the era of the Third Reich.* German democracy was dead. But with nearly six million unemployed, Germany had only a lukewarm devotion to democracy anyway.

The Nazi appeal contained a lot of idealism. The idea of living in a strong, virile country appealed to everyone, particularly the young.

---

*The first German empire (or Reich) was considered to be the Holy Roman Empire; the second, the German Empire from 1871 to 1919.

Everyone was wide open to the propaganda that assured relief from depression, inflation, and other tremendous hardships, and Nazism promised a near welfare state. Hitler was totally underrated by his opponents. The Communist and Social Democratic parties felt sure his incompetence would quickly be revealed and that the Nazis would topple with little impact. Hardly anyone expected the Third Reich to burn its swastika across Europe's landscape.

Early in 1933, massive book burnings destroyed once and for all the books containing opposing ideologies and philosophies. All that was free and joyful quickly vanished. Only one enthusiasm was permitted: enthusiasm for Hitler.

Suspicion was the new order of the day. Later it was revealed that Hitler was suspicious of even his closest associates. He had come into full power through the fists and guns of his Nazi storm troopers. Clearly, the law and Hitler were one.

Later in the year, all other political parties were forbidden in Germany. The newly established secret police, the Gestapo, were given complete freedom to be ruthless, which would epitomize its character during the next twelve years in Germany. Eventually everything would suffer in Nazi Germany: religion, education, industry, business, and most of all, human rights. Hitler swore he would never leave the chancellery in his lifetime.

To insure this, he immediately enrolled a bodyguard of forty thousand men. A particularly sadistic group of men who were a law unto themselves, this organization was called *Schutzstaffel* (literally, "protective rank")—abbreviated SS. Many of them were the dregs of society—the unemployed, drifters, perverts, and ex-prisoners. They viewed their job of being SS henchmen as a path to riches and a way to avoid real work. Overnight they rose from beer hall patrons to men with power, and that power went to their heads. Both Hitler and his SS men wanted a law to do without the law, and they soon had it.

The Gestapo were all members of the SS. Their duties were similar to those of the SS, and they were equally corrupt and power hungry. They all moved ahead by force, taking over government buildings, hoisting the swastika flag everywhere, and arresting any government official who opposed Hitler. President Hindenburg went along with everything except the persecution of the Jews. He even signed a decree in 1933 that freed all Nazis from prisons.

Every Nazi opponent or suspicious individual would be exterminated or driven out of the country. The lucky ones made it to safety, though they were few. Everything associated with the Jews would be the brunt of a particularly vicious attack, starting slowly in 1933 and culminating in an attempt at genocide, or race annihilation. Hitler even had the Reichstag building burned to the ground in 1933 because it reminded him of a synagogue. In the spring, a boycott was ordered against Jewish businesses and professions to force them to pay large indemnities to maintain their bare existence.

That same year, an unfamiliar term gained prominence in the world's language of despair: *concentration camp*. At first crude, primitive, and poorly run, in time concentration camps would become shrewdly run businesses that housed millions of Jews, Christians, and political opponents, as well as all the sick, insane, and elderly—including Germans. Hitler thought these groups were threatening the purity of the Aryan race. The camps were to become Mother's and my home. Only by hanging tightly to Jesus' hand would our journey into hell be bearable.

* * *

"We'll get you after school, you little Jew brat," came the menacing voice behind me in my first-grade class. I pretended I didn't hear and gave full attention to my teacher, even though moments earlier she too had humiliated me. Even my near-blonde hair couldn't hide my Jewishness, for my mother, Hella, and I had to register our race at a nearby district office. The names of the non-Aryans had been sent immediately to the schools and other places, resulting in our being watched carefully and subjected to varying degrees of persecution.

Hella, Mother, and Anita (6 years old), 1934

In addition, Hella and I were the only children at our school who were not members of the Hitler Youth organization. They were nothing but a uniformed bunch of young robots proudly wearing their drab outfits and swastikas and mouthing, "Heil Hitler" enthusiastically wherever they went. Many of them took special delight in making life miserable for a Jewish child. For some reason they singled me out much more than Hella—perhaps because I was so small and helpless. But Mother had strictly instructed us never to hit back because the Gestapo could retaliate and haul us off to jail. It was difficult for me as a child to understand Hitler, this demagogue whose picture was everywhere—in our classroom, on street banners, and, later, even defiling church altars.

Each morning my teacher, Fräulein (Miss) Kinzel, would pray toward the picture of Hitler. Her words still ring in my ears: "Dear God, protect our dear leader. Make him strong. Let us all learn to love him. May he have many years of glorious reign." All of us had to fold our hands and bow our heads. Then we had to raise our arms in the proper Heil Hitler manner and sing the German national anthem with great gusto. Failure to follow this nationalistic ritual meant a beating or being turned over to the Gestapo. Whenever I met Fräulein Kinzel, I gave her the Nazi salute and muttered some words, but I never really uttered an official Heil Hitler.

A birthday card arrived from Father on my seventh birthday, after we hadn't heard from him for more than a year. He explained that he had been sentenced to jail because of his involvement in the Social Democratic Party. Later he escaped from prison and fled to Prague, but he was captured again. Now he was accusing Mother of betraying his whereabouts, but we had no idea to where he had disappeared. He was free now, but the Nazis had ordered him to divorce Mother because she was Jewish.

"Mother, Father wants to see Hella and me at his mother's in south Breslau." My voice was filled with cautious excitement, yet I felt anger at some of his accusations.

"You cannot trust him, Anita," Mother replied. "The Nazis may have brainwashed him like everyone else. But you may go if you wish. However, you must watch every word you say, because he may be our enemy now. Jews are picked up every day on trumped-up charges or because they oppose the Nazis. Tell your father that you aren't against the Nazis in spite of everything. Do you understand?"

Some Jews and other persons suspected of being against Hitler's regime were already being sent off to camps or prisons. However, in 1934 many of these people were released quickly and allowed to return home.

I found it difficult to dredge up any affection for Father. He had abandoned us, saying he could not help us financially. Actually, he knew the German court would never force him to help us because Mother was Jewish. The law was on his side, and he took full advantage of it. But Hella and I began to ride the streetcar twice a month to the other end of Breslau to see Father.

Occasionally he slipped us each a small amount of money. He insisted that he hated the Nazis and that his political sentiment still belonged to the defunct Social Democrats. He did all the talking—almost monotonously so. A dozen times over, he told us stories about World War I, his flashing blue Aryan eyes zeroing in on Hella and looking right through me as though I didn't exist. To ease my hurt I retreated into my own world and drew pictures during our visits. But the visits made summer vacation pass a little more quickly. Perhaps my hunger for a father's attention prodded me to take the hour-long ride, followed by a mile-long walk, to see him. Or perhaps it was just a temporary diversion from the unpleasantness of Nazi Germany in 1934—from the stones and abuses hurled at me by the German children.

The most precious time for me was the time I spent with Mother. Eventually she would be forced to do heavy manual labor, hauling manure for long, hot hours before dragging her aching body home at night. But Nazi Germany was still young, and her leaders' diabolical minds were still scheming for worse times ahead. Persecution was present but bearable.

Our little radio was our most precious possession, for it kept us one step ahead of the plans of the Gestapo and Hitler. Mother awakened us unusually early one hot, sticky August morning in 1934.

"Anita! Hella!" she exclaimed with fear in her voice. "President Hindenburg has died. It is not good. He was against the persecution of the Jews!"

Sleepily we sat up in bed and gazed at Mother. Though Hella was only eleven and I was only seven, Mother talked to us as if we were adults. She assumed we understood the ramifications of Nazi Germany; and perhaps God did give us understanding far beyond our years.

"You must take every precaution," Mother continued. "Keep to yourselves and never utter anything against the Nazis. Don't trust anyone. Do you hear?" We nodded our understanding.

Mother paced our tiny one-room apartment. "All Hitler talks about is the pure German race; it is an obsession with him. He screams and his face is contorted with violence and emotion. Everywhere the crowds roar their approval, but he looks at them with contempt."

Legally there should have been an election for a new president. But Hitler was not in the mood for an election, so he simply abolished the title and the office of the presidency, appointing himself *der Führer*, "the Leader." He also named himself commander in chief of the army.

However, the German people were invited to register their approval of his actions. Nearly 88 percent of the population said they were pleased, and then Hitler was in complete control.

All Jews were deprived of their civic rights in 1935, and the Law for the Protection of German Blood and German Honor was issued. Again it was hammered home to the Aryans that they must maintain and protect the purity of their German blood. Marriages between Jews and Germans were forbidden, and some marriages were annulled. Jews were not allowed to display the German flag.

That winter most of our non-Jewish friends told us they could no longer associate with us. A few would visit us bravely in the middle of the night. I overheard one dear friend of Mother's saying, "Hilde, you know we still love you. You must understand. We oppose the Nazis, but they are threatening our lives if we are kind to the Jews. You'll have to break it to Anita that our little Gunther can no longer play with her. I know how disappointed she will be."

Mother knew too. Even the midnight visits of friends bringing baskets of food to compensate for our pitiful rations couldn't compensate for the loss of my friendship with Gunther.

My teacher was still Fräulein Kinzel, who continued to make school unbearable. She openly hated me for not being a member of the Hitler Youth, and she delighted in hitting me with a ruler on the back of my head or hands. Teachers were allowed to spank children who were a discipline problem or who didn't keep up with assignments. She made full use of those rights with me, always exaggerating my failures.

Three times a week our class went to another room for religion studies, where I could learn more about Jesus. It was a breath of fresh spring air in a howling blizzard of disappointments. Jesus began occupying more and more of my thoughts and attention. I learned that His life was a paradox and His death wasn't final. He taught that by dying we really live, and by giving away we gain. Years later I would hear Him called "the hound of heaven." Indeed, it seemed if He was following me in a loving and protecting way, not for selfish reasons,

Anita's Mother, Hilde

but because He wanted to give me a gift.

Finally, Mother was forced to do heavy labor to earn her pitiful welfare money. All day long she did manual labor, and Hella and I were left alone until evening. We were given a hot meal at a nearby Catholic day care that still dared show an ounce of kindness to a Jew, but I could hardly eat. My lonely heart ached for Mother's company, and Hella began retreating into a world of books and philosophy. Mother dragged herself home after dark and spent the evening repairing our worn-out, hand-me-down clothing. Mother and I talked about God a lot, while Hella buried her nose in a book.

"Which God do you pray to, Mother?" I asked enthusiastically.

"Oh, just any God. Whichever one is listening. I don't know whose God it is—the Jews' God or the Gentiles' God. I don't know if it's Jesus or Buddha or Muhammad. You pray to Jesus if you want, if it makes you feel better."

"Oh, Mother, it does! I just know Jesus hears me. Have you ever prayed to Jesus, Mother?"

"Once I did, I think. I don't know, though, a lot of Jews have been killed by people bearing His name."

In spite of our poverty, Mother made birthdays and Christmases special for Hella and me. We always received a gift, even if its worth was only a penny or two. At Christmas that year, I particularly strained to hear the carols coming from the church steeple several blocks away. The birth of Jesus had a special meaning to me for some reason. How strange to have such a friend as Jesus. We'd never met, but His presence was unmistakable. "The Christmas carols from the church steeple are telling Jesus' story, Mother!" I exclaimed with delight. "I know the words to the carol. I learned them at the Catholic day-care center. Could I sing them?"

Mother smiled while I carried on in festive merriment. It was a brief interlude in the absurdity of life in Nazi Germany.

And so life crept slowly on. Some weeks it dragged mercilessly because I'd been cut off from my friends and Mother was gone until evening. Except for religion class, school continued to be unbearable.

2

race disgrace

the forest just outside of Breslau was alive with the color and fragrance of spring in 1937 as I walked over a mile to the Bethany Lutheran Parochial School. I was now in the fifth grade and ten years old. I had had to pass a strict entrance exam to get into Bethany. Because Hella was a student there, I could attend at no extra cost as long as I passed the exams. Father had consented to pay Hella's tuition. He never would have done so for me; he would have been just as happy to see my education end at the fourth grade. How I had prayed that Jesus would help me pass those tests.

Our teachers were wonderful Lutheran deaconesses who were kind to all of us. Because I now felt loved rather than threatened and intimidated, I blossomed out as an excellent student, surprising everyone, including Mother and Hella.

No German national anthems and "Heil Hitlers" were heard at Bethany. Morning devotions excluded any reference to the Führer. No scowling pictures of him were displayed, and as of yet, none of the children belonged to the Hitler Youth. For me it was an oasis in the desert of anti-Semitism, which allowed me to regain some sense of worth as well as to explore further the teachings of Jesus.

Even more exciting than our Lutheran school was hearing

about St. Barbara's Lutheran Church in Breslau that spring. The pastor, Ernst Hornig, and his assistant, Vicar Kathe Staritz, were especially interested in helping Jewish believers. They also desired to win Jews to Christ and then help them leave Germany. (We heard about the church from a converted Jewish family in our building.) Even Mother consented to visit the church because of that faint prospect of freedom.

Since the church was located in a poor district of Breslau, it would require a long streetcar ride both ways. But a glimmer of freedom made any condition bearable, so Mother, Hella, and I journeyed to the church one spring Sunday in 1937. Now I could hear about Jesus in school all week long and at church on Sundays too. I couldn't believe God's goodness!

Pastor Hornig became a substitute father for me. A graying man in his forties, he supported his own six children on his meager income. Whenever he talked about the Jews, tears welled up in his eyes. Of course, his insight was far beyond my understanding as a child.

Mother and Hella consented to attend church each week and learn more about Jesus. Maybe Mother was only using the church as a means to get us all out of the country, but nevertheless Jesus would have an opportunity to touch her.

Whenever I met Pastor Hornig, his gentle gray eyes looked down at me lovingly. But those same eyes reflected fear, for the pastor had the premonition that his homeland was about to be bathed in blood. Yet he spoke

Hella, Mother, and Anita (9 years old)

with compassion about Hitler and his roaming bands of SS men and Gestapo. He urged us to pray that the Spirit of God would touch their lives.

Soon Gestapo agents dressed in plain clothes visited the church services. Nevertheless, Pastor Hornig knew who they were. We had heard that one of the leading Protestant churchmen in Germany was heading a movement to harmonize Christianity with Nazi beliefs, including anti-Semitism, to the extent of leaving the Old Testament out of Christian teachings because of its Jewishness. Pastor Hornig said the new Nazi church would be called the German Christian Church. Some German Protestant pastors would sell out to it, but most refused and then helped organize the Confessional Evangelical Church, which would continue to preach the whole Bible, including the gospel of Jesus and the important role of the Jewish people in God's eternal plan. It also would oppose having Hitler's picture placed on church altars.

My life took on new dimensions. I was loved and accepted by my teachers, classmates, Pastor Hornig, and Vicar Staritz; my spiritual appetite was being fed; and we now had a ray of hope, for we felt that Pastor Hornig would ultimately provide a way for us to escape the nightmare that lay ahead for Nazi Germany.

"Don't forget to talk to Jesus about even the smallest need, Anita," Pastor Hornig reminded me one morning after we left church. "He's never too busy to listen, and He cares about all our problems, not just the big ones." The noon sun was especially bright that day, and I had to squint into it as I gazed up at Pastor Hornig.

"I've talked to Jesus since I was six years old, Pastor," I replied.

Mother and Hella were walking ahead, but I hung behind, hungry for even a second more of this man's warmth and attention. "Jesus is my best Friend."

"But is He your Savior, too, Anita?" the pastor questioned as he bent over slightly, looking intently into my eyes. "Have you really asked Him into your life to be your loving heavenly Father and the Savior for your sins?"

"I don't know," I confessed awkwardly. Then I replied enthusiastically, "But if I haven't, I want to do it!"

St. Barbara's Lutheran Church in Breslau

"Then just ask Him, Anita. It's that simple. Ask Jesus to be your Savior today. Tomorrow may be too late. And He has promised eternal life to all those who receive Him. Then He will never leave you nor forsake you. He'll always be your Comforter and Protector, no matter how bad things get. Remember that, Anita, even when things worsen here in Germany, when all is black and uncertain and you feel utterly alone. If you have Jesus in your heart, He will get you through anything."

Mother beckoned me, lest we miss the streetcar, so I said farewell to this man I'd grown to love so much. I ran down the street but looked back several times to see Pastor Hornig waving to me, a special smile on his face that I was sure was reserved just for me. It was the happiest day of my short life, for on the way home I asked Jesus to come into my life in a new and special way. I knew He did, that He was closer to me than ever before, and that He would always be by my side.

The next day a radio announcer said Hitler planned to shut all parochial schools because they didn't include Nazism and they allowed Jews to attend. No date was given for the closings. Again, stern warnings were given to Germans who helped Jews in any way. Christians who helped Jews would be subject to special reprisals, including time in a concentration camp. I knew my glorious days at the Lutheran school were coming to a swift conclusion.

* * *

Annoying radio static jarred me from a sound sleep one gray March morning in 1938. With glowing terms of praise for the Führer, the announcer proclaimed that Austria was now a part of the German Reich. Hitler had always desired to restore his homeland to the Reich, so he sent two hundred thousand German soldiers over the border to seize Austria. Now seven million more German citizens could bolster the German army.

"Germany will be at war soon," Mother said as I still lay in bed.

It was so cold that morning I didn't care if I ever got up. Our tiny, coal-burning furnace did an inadequate job, and we had to carefully ration our limited coal supply because we could barely afford it.

My Lutheran school still had not been closed, but it was just a matter of time. Perhaps Hitler was too preoccupied with war plans to worry about the schools that accepted Jews and treated them kindly, although that didn't seem like him. Meanwhile, I basked each day in God's goodness to me. I loved my teachers, the church, and Pastor Hornig.

Mother was becoming more and more silent, for she seemed to have a barometer within her that sensed impending danger. Some might have flippantly called her a prophet of doom, but actually, she was realistic and nearly always right. She showed signs of spiritual growth every day. Now she never missed Pastor Hornig's midweek Bible study, even though she had to ride the streetcar late at night in order to attend. The pastor had given each of us a Bible, and I watched Mother carry hers proudly out the door each week. If it was snowing, she wrapped it carefully so the thin pages would not get wet. Hours after Hella and I went to bed, she sat quietly in her rocking chair, reading the Bible. In spite of my ragged clothes, near-starvation rations, and all the absurdity of life in Nazi Germany, I was extremely happy. Was this the peace that Pastor Hornig had told me would result from Jesus living in my heart?

We still had hopes of leaving Germany, for Pastor Hornig worked every day to find a place to which Mother, Hella, and I could escape. He was sure it was just a matter of time. Thousands of Jews were leaving the country, so why not us? Before emigration was stopped, three hundred thousand fortunate people found freedom in other lands. Germany allowed them to leave because the Nazis wanted to show the world that Jews could not possibly be Germans. Thus, a new phrase cropped up, which was really just a new term for an old problem: *race disgrace.*

* * *

Hitler still had not closed down Bethany School by the fall, so one afternoon I hurried home from school as usual. Hella had left a while before me and would be home already. I had picked out a special route so that few other children could spot me, and I wouldn't get beaten up. Walks home in the warm sunshine were pleasant those days, and I could take time to talk to God and thank Him for His bountiful gifts to me and my family.

I watched proud Germans scurry about the city of Breslau, no doubt dreaming that the Führer was reestablishing the glorious Germany they once knew or had read about. Everywhere I looked, Hitler's picture and the swastika were painted, and the German flag flapped in the breeze. An ominous sensation shot through me every time I saw these things.

Suddenly Hella was racing down the street to meet me as I entered our block, panic and fear written all over her face. Her body shook visibly, and her face was contorted because she was about to break into tears. Curious people stared at Hella, but they kept moving, afraid to get involved. I sensed even before she spoke that disaster had struck our home.

"Mother's been taken!" she gasped. "She was sent home from work, and the Gestapo were there when I came home from school." Even though Hella was breathless, I tried to make her talk more rapidly. As we hurried down the block, I was filled with questions I didn't have time to ask.

"The Gestapo emptied every drawer, looking for some kind of evidence against Mother," Hella continued, tears streaming down her face. "They couldn't find anything, so they grabbed her and threw her in a police car. Did you hear the siren wailing? It was Mother they were taking!"

We cautiously entered our apartment, which was in absolute ruin. No drawer was left unemptied. Everything we owned had been strewn about the house and examined for evidence. "They couldn't find what they were looking for," Hella said, "so they trumped up a charge. They said they had been informed that Father stayed here last night and that he committed race disgrace. Can you believe it? Anita, they've taken her to jail!"

As I searched for words to comfort my fifteen-year-old sister, I prayed silently that Jesus would strengthen and comfort us. Hadn't Pastor Hornig said that Jesus would always give us the strength we needed? "God will bring her back safely, Hella. I know He will. Will you believe Him for it with me?"

"I think God is a figment of your imagination!" Hella shouted angrily.

"Hella!" I protested. "He is all we have!"

"He's an illusion," Hella insisted. "Not God or anyone else will ever get us out of Germany. Don't fool yourself, Anita. Even if there is a God, not even He looks favorably on the Jews."

We paced and pondered. Mother had been picked up at two o'clock that afternoon. If it was a brief interrogation, she could be home by suppertime. But if they enforced the false charges and sentenced her, it could be weeks or months before we'd see her again. Did I dare use a neighbor's phone and call Pastor Hornig? But there was nothing he could do, anyway, and he would have to take the long streetcar ride to our house.

The hours passed slowly. As it began to get dark, Hella despaired again and buried her sobbing face in her pillow. I didn't want my words to sound silly to her, so I sat quietly beside her, searching for the wisdom of an adult. The clock ticking next to us was all we heard, and its hands moved mercilessly slow. We listened intently for Mother's footsteps or the sound of her key in the door, forgetting about eating dinner and the impossible idea of doing our schoolwork. Hella withdrew again to her own secret world, where she spent so much time. I had a secret world, too, but in it I sat silently pleading with Jesus to bail us out of this trouble.

Shortly after midnight, we heard the familiar steps. Mother was home! White with fear and fatigue, she struggled in the front door. She had been forced to stand up ten hours while being interrogated, with no break and no food. Surely Jesus had delivered her out of the lion's den!

"I am on the blacklist now," she said quietly. "I will be watched nearly every day. If I do the slightest questionable thing, I can be taken to prison. You girls might be watched too." A particular hurt look overcame her as she dropped exhausted into a chair. "You tell your father never to come near our apartment. For a Jew to be with a German is an abomination. Do you understand?" Actually, Father hadn't been near our apartment at any time. The Nazi charge was completely phony.

We nodded our heads, though. We understood perfectly.

* * *

A month later, in November 1938, a young Polish Jew shot an official of the German embassy in Paris. Now Hitler would pour gasoline on the smoldering fires of his anti-Semitic campaign, and Jews everywhere would feel its effect.

A frantic knock sounded on our door early one morning. It was our elderly neighbor, a lovely Christian lady who had a special love for our family.

"Hilde! Hilde!" came the desperate voice in a whisper.

Mother opened the door a crack and saw the frightened face of Mrs. Schmidt.

"Hilde, they're burning all the synagogues! They say it's in retaliation for the killing of the German embassy official in Paris. You must not go anywhere. If you need anything, I'll try to get it for you."

"So it has finally happened," Mother replied, without inviting Mrs. Schmidt in. It was too dangerous to bring her into the apartment, because she might be accused of aiding a Jew.

"Yes, Hilde. Even Jews on our block are being dragged out of their homes. They're taking just the men now, but the women will go in time. Now that you're on the blacklist, you must be careful. I'm praying for you and the girls, Hilde. I'll hide you if I have to."

"Don't be foolish! They would kill you."

"God can still work a miracle, Hilde. Every day of life in Germany is a miracle. I must go now."

The sirens blared all that day and night. We sat by the radio, hoping to keep ahead of the Gestapo. Most of the synagogues would be left to burn to the ground as the Germans and Nazis watched unaffected. They felt that Jews were getting what they deserved.

Over a four-day period, thousands of Jewish men were picked

View of a burning synagogue. *Courtesy United States Holocaust Memorial Museum*

up and taken to unknown destinations, leaving bewildered families behind. Some would be interrogated or tortured for a few weeks, then allowed to return home. Others were sent to Buchenwald and other work camps for hard labor. It seemed to be a random selection and sentencing. Nothing made much sense, especially the false charges against the innocent victims and their families. We watched some of the chaos on the street below our building. Old men were being dragged away by their beards and thrown into trucks so crowded that they could hardly breathe. Their families gasped in horror. In some cases, a teenage son was the only one taken. Mother and I prayed silently for the victims and their loved ones.

We remained huddled in our apartment for five days until the sirens stopped and the synagogues lay in smoldering ruins. Nazi hate propaganda poured over the airwaves, saying that the Jews were finally getting their just punishment, and that more was in store. Eventually all of Germany would be *judenrein* ("cleansed of Jews").

"Jews are strictly forbidden to attend concerts and other forms of public entertainment," came the harsh voice over the radio. "A complete list of restrictions will be aired later as they are handed down from our Führer. A Jew caught violating any restriction will suffer the severest punishment."

Little by little, we received word from friends and relatives. Each of them had either a son, brother, husband, or father taken by the Nazis. Now agonizing weeks of uncertainty lay ahead. Some loved ones would never return. Others would come back weeks or months later with a host of nervous disorders from the mental and physical strain. Frequently those who were picked up were intellectuals or scholars, for whom Hitler's SS men and the Gestapo had a particular hatred. Hitler's henchmen, uneducated and below average in intelligence, despised even those men who wore glasses. A list of the educated intellectuals was available, and those men received the brunt of the first attack. The immediate men in charge of the SS included Heinrich Himmler, Reinhard Heydrich, and Adolf Eichmann. All three names would become synonymous with cold-blooded terror.

Hella continued to despair because of her lack of faith in God. Now even Mother tried to comfort her with passages from the Bible that she had learned from Pastor Hornig.

"Hella, Pastor Hornig is in touch with an organization that wants to help us. It is called the Help Organization for Christian Non-Aryans and Christian Jews. He says they are hoping to send us all to England very soon, and that the church will help with our expenses. We must all pray that this can be done quickly. Germany doesn't have much time left."

And so we prayed every day that the process could be speeded up and that a way would be made for our emigration. God had led His people out of Pharaoh's death grip; He could free us too. As long as we had hope, we could endure anything.

* * *

Dear Mrs. Dittman:

We regret to inform you that you are being evicted from your apartment. This is an attempt to purify this neighborhood. You are being sent to a Jewish neighborhood where a room has been secured for you. You have twenty days to report to 1298 Van Duesen Street. Failure to comply within this twenty-day period will result in serious reprisals. . . .

Mother's voice sounded grave as she read us the note. "'Jewish neighborhood' is a nice term for 'ghetto,'" she said. "It is in the middle of the city. I know the address. It is rat-infested and dilapidated. At least we will be nearer Pastor Hornig and the church. You girls will have a long ride to school. Well, no doubt Hitler will close it soon, anyhow."

"It's all right, Mother," I replied, searching for words.

"I think the Eric Sandbergs are the caretakers there," Mother said, trying to look on a brighter side. "I knew them years ago. They are a nice Jewish family, and their sons, Rudy and Ernest, are about your age. Maybe you will have some playmates again." As I studied

Mother's face, I saw how she had aged ten years in the last few years.

"We cannot afford to move our furniture," she added. "We will have to sell all but the essentials—even your stuffed animals, Anita. I'm sorry." I cringed but I would never let Mother see. She already had enough trouble to break her heart.

"And we'll have to leave your books behind too, Hella. We all must sacrifice."

It would be even harder to say good-bye to some friends in our building. A few of them still had missing loved ones.

We heard another knock on our door. Mother opened the door, only to look down at a haggard, elderly woman who was a dwarf. The woman leaned awkwardly on a cane and shook visibly from the cold in our unheated halls.

"Could I sell you some thread today?" she pleaded with both her voice and her eyes.

Without hesitating, Mother invited the old woman in. We saw that she was wrapped in three torn scarves and bundled in a torn and ragged coat. She had no overshoes, and her thin shoes were snow covered. Her gloveless hands were red and cracked. "Won't you come in?" Mother encouraged. "I'll give you a cup of hot chocolate."

I watched the old woman's face light up. She hobbled through the door, carrying a small knapsack containing the odds and ends that she peddled.

"Can I serve you some food?" Mother insisted. We knew that whatever Mother gave her would be our next day's food rations. It was hard to express Christian charity when it came down to our limited food rations. Mother didn't even wait for the old lady's reply. Instead she gave her a slice of bread and a small bowl of vegetables, and Hella and I watched our next day's meal being consumed hungrily. Then Mother took out a few pennies to buy some thread from her. Finally she sent the woman off with her own gloves.

"What will we eat tomorrow?" I questioned nervously.

"God will return it," Mother said. "Pastor Hornig says God will double what we give away, Anita."

The next day Mrs. Schmidt came back to see us. "Hilde," she announced as she pushed her way through our door, carrying a bundle of food, "God laid it upon my heart to bring you this food today." The aroma of homemade soup, freshly baked bread, and some fruit nearly sent us into ecstasy. She had brought us enough for several meals. God had more than doubled the amount of food Mother had given away, and her faith in God took a giant step forward that day.

* * *

Two days after Christmas, we moved to our new location. We'd given away nearly all our possessions. I truly left my childhood behind, but then I'd not had much of an opportunity to be a child in Germany anyway. I buried my tears so Mother wouldn't see them. Instead, we all tried to talk hopefully.

"Well, when we go to England, we will have to leave everything behind anyway," I announced, quickly brushing away a tear.

Eric and Rosa Sandberg greeted us at the door of our new home. Their son Rudy was fifteen, and Ernest was seventeen. The Sandbergs, who were Orthodox Jews, were old friends of Mother's, and Mother was afraid they would not accept us now that we believed in Jesus. But they proved to be loving and accepting people. They shared the Passover and other Jewish holidays with us; since Mother, Hella, and I spoke some Yiddish, we could still fit in well. They made our adjustment more bearable. Hella and Ernest became inseparable, and Rudy and I were good friends, even though he was four years older than I.

Our new home was a two-hundred-year-old brownstone structure. Blasts of cold air came through the cracked windows. Our one room had no refrigerator, so we had to buy our food daily, requiring a lengthy wait in line.

We carried coal up from the basement for the inadequate heater and hung our laundry line across our one room. We had one tub for washing our dishes, our clothes, and our bodies. We shared a tiny bathroom with other families, and we took turns using a tiny two-burner stove with another family. They had first priority with cooking, so we frequently ate dinner late at night. The worst inconvenience, however, was the pesky bedbugs that infested our room, making a restful night's sleep impossible.

That winter the Nazis took another step in degrading the Jew. In Hitler's opinion, the most dangerous Jews were those whose Jewishness was not obvious. They might be assimilating themselves into German society. Thus, all Jews were forced to wear a yellow Star of David on their clothing in

A Star of David patch worn by Jews during Nazi occupation. *Courtesy United States Holocaust Memorial Museum*

order to be easily identified. Mother protested loudly to the Gestapo, demanding they exclude her because her husband was a German and all of us believed in Jesus. Miraculously, the Gestapo gave us a temporary stay, but they reminded us that we were still considered Jews and therefore had to obey the same restrictions as other Jews.

However, each of the Sandbergs had a bright, yellow star sewn on all their clothing. Consequently, they seldom left the building because the star incited various kinds of persecution.

We pressed on optimistically, feeling assured that it was just a matter of time before our flight to freedom in England.

3

tRappeD

War clouds hung lower over Germany early in 1939, and we prayed again for a swift miracle of freedom. We had learned that it was not just Jews who were being persecuted, for Hitler had slowly been exterminating Germany's sick, elderly, insane, and mentally incompetent as part of his plan to build a perfect Aryan race.

Now the newspaper frequently printed the word *Judenrein* ("clean of Jews") as town after town rid itself of its Jewish population. Each town wiped its hands clean as the last "dirty Jew" finally was run out or sent off to a camp. Millions more Jews were crowded into filthy ghettos.

Finally, the Führer lived up to his promise and closed the parochial schools. My heart sank, for that meant public school again, providing we could even raise the tuition. Then the onslaught of persecution would begin again for me. Even my faith in Jesus could not overcome my despondency for several days, for I knew that the abuse would be a hundred times worse than it had been a few years ago.

More disastrous news came: The Nazis burned the office of the Help Organization for Christian Non-Aryans and Christian Jews. In the process, they destroyed all the files; we had to reapply, with more long months of waiting.

The ghetto existence, the bad news, and now the public school experience merged into a bad waking dream. My public school teachers were nothing but Nazi robot teaching machines, and the schoolbooks had been rewritten and filled with propaganda. We had to stand at attention and enthusiastically shout, "Heil Hitler!" Though Pastor Hornig paid my tuition, we could not afford schoolbooks, nor would the school give me any. Thus, I could not keep up with assignments; soon my grades tumbled. Teachers took advantage of the situation by ridiculing me constantly in front of the class.

My life, just like Nazi Germany itself, was a jumbled mixture of highs and lows. Rudy and Ernest were able to find safety in England, and their departure day was filled with joyful tears.

Mother, Hella, the Sandbergs, and I all expected to reunite with them in London in a few months; but the Sandbergs were never to make it beyond Camp Theresienstadt.

Anita was 12 in this photo; Hella was almost 17—1939

Then we received word that our papers were being processed and the inevitable escape would be soon. We were frantic with anticipation, for we expected to have our visas and passports by July. We worked feverishly on our English and endured all the other hardships with greater ease, knowing that anything is bearable if it has an end.

By early July, every day found me perched on our doorstep hours before the postman was due. Maybe today would be the day he would bring our passports to freedom! The wait was unbearable as the month crawled along, but finally, on the last day of July we received that official-looking envelope. This had to be it! I grabbed it from the postman and nearly broke my neck racing up the stairs to find Mother . . .

But now we knew that only Hella would escape to England. *Mother and I were indeed trapped!*

By fall the war began in earnest. Germany surged ahead, optimistic because of her swift victory in Poland. The frighteningly diabolical trio of Adolf Eichmann, Reinhard Heydrich, and Heinrich Himmler was ordered to find a "final solution to the Jewish problem," and it was generally understood that the final solution meant total extermination.

Auschwitz and Dachau, two of the deadlier camps, would strike similar terror within the Jews of Europe. Rudolf Ross was put in charge of the genocide at Auschwitz. Upon his orders, two thousand Jews would be gassed at one time. As men, women, and children were shoved together into massive "shower rooms," some were stamped on their chests with a coded number that indicated they had gold teeth. When they finally realized they weren't taking a shower, they screamed and cried for mercy, but their cries fell on deaf ears. Amused guards watched through peepholes as they suffered and died. Hideous horror stories began to trickle out of the various camps, putting unbearable pressure on European Jews, who knew that they were all potential gas-chamber victims.

In 1939, Germans began experiencing a fear of their own as the country scurried for air-raid shelters. Bombs weren't falling on Germany yet, but drills had begun. Homes and businesses complied with blackout regulations, and planes frequently raced across the German sky that fall, though without dropping any deadly weapons.

Rising costs for tuition and schoolbooks and the increased anti-Semitism made my school life miserable and my future education questionable. In addition, home conditions were difficult. Two of Mother's sisters had come to live with us in our one room, and we had to share the kitchen and bath with additional families.

Mother's sisters—Aunt Friede and Aunt Elsbeth—were endlessly annoyed at my strong faith in Jesus and Mother's growing interest in Him. Their nagging, coupled with the unbearable bedbugs in our apartment, made life a chore. I gave Aunt Elsbeth my bed and slept on a lumpy, bedbug-infested sofa, falling asleep each night while arguments rang through the room. Aunt Elsbeth insisted I had deliberately planted bedbugs in her bed just to torment her.

I was now twelve and about to enter early teen years; living in Nazi Germany only added to my difficulties. Often, as the lights went out at night, I lapsed into self-pity and cried myself to sleep. I knew it would be a long winter with minimum food rations; crowded, substandard living quarters; and that never-ending dread of the Gestapo knock on the door. More and more Jews feared venturing into the streets. Though Mother and I had still been able to avoid wearing the terrible yellow Star of David that revealed our heritage, the fact remained that the Gestapo knew every Jew in the city. And Breslau had a reputation as a strong pro-Hitler, anti-Semitic center.

We hardly dared go to Pastor Hornig's church. The macabre scenes we saw on the way caused bad dreams at night as our subconscious minds relived what we had seen: Jews by the hundreds being herded into trucks as they stared glassy-eyed with fear at being separated from loved ones. Since we were in a Jewish ghetto, we could look out our window almost any day and see such scenes on the street below. The more we were identified as Jewish Christians attending a Protestant church, the more free time we were given, but now that two "religious Jews"—Aunt Friede and Aunt Elsbeth—lived with Mother and me, some of our built-in protection vanished.

Finally, after falling hopelessly behind in school that winter because I wasn't able to obtain textbooks, I dropped out.

4

"a LoveLy chRIStIaN..."

Pastor Hornig, our one faithful friend and contact with the sane world, brought me some heartening news in the early spring of 1940. "Anita," he said in a fatherly way, "I've been in touch with a Mrs. Michaelis in Berlin. She is married to a Jewish Christian lawyer who just fled Germany for Shanghai. Her two sons have escaped to London, and she's desperately lonely for a child around the house. If you will go and live with her, she says she will pay for all your education in Berlin. It might be a little safer for you in Berlin, so I think you should consider it."

I looked at Mother, but she would give me no hint of her feelings. Obviously, she wanted it to be my decision, though separation would mean more sadness for both of us. My aunts paced nervously, hoping I would accept the offer so there would be more room in the dingy apartment.

"She's a wealthy lady," Pastor Hornig continued, "so you would get the proper food you need. She has a nice apartment in Berlin, and she says she will let you come home frequently to visit your mother. I think she is a lovely Christian, Anita. You should try to make life in Germany bearable for yourself until we can get you out."

I would learn that it was one of his few misjudgments.

As I weakly nodded my approval, a flood of fears engulfed me—fear of the unknown, of leaving Mother, and that one of us might get picked up by the Gestapo without the other knowing. They were fears that no one other than Jesus could fully comprehend, fears no twelve-year-old should have to deal with.

"I'll go," I said quietly, almost in a whisper.

"Good," Pastor Hornig replied. "I'll make the arrangements immediately. You can plan on leaving early next week, Anita. Mrs. Michaelis will send you the train ticket. She's so anxious to meet you. She said she has always wanted a daughter."

Skepticism permeated every inch of my body. What person in her right mind would want to take on the problems associated with being identified with the Jews?

"You will look after Mother, won't you?" I asked the pastor.

"Of course," he replied enthusiastically. Seeing that I wasn't convinced about the decision, Pastor Hornig continued to persuade me of the wisdom of my move.

"Anita," he said compassionately, "I am going to continue to do everything I can to get you out of Germany. Hitler doesn't make many mistakes in the war, but when he does, he makes the Jews pay for it. He blames the Jews over and over again for starting this war. Breslau is one of the centers of Hitler's support, but he still is letting a few Jews leave the country. If there is a way for you and your mother to leave, I will find it."

With those comforting words of hoped-for freedom, Pastor Hornig left the apartment.

I tossed on my lumpy sofa all night. Warm woolen blankets, clean sheets, proper food, and an education couldn't replace Mother, whose absence in my life was almost unthinkable. We would be separated by so many miles—what if she were arrested? And just how much safer could Berlin be than Breslau? Berlin was three times as large, which meant three times as many Gestapo agents to pick

Courtesy United States Holocaust Memorial Museum

me up and send me to Auschwitz. Somehow I had to put all of the unknowns and fears into Jesus' hands. He would have to help me choke back the flood of tears I felt coming and soothe my aching heart at the thought of separation.

I soon wondered how Pastor Hornig's judgment could have been so wrong. Mrs. Michaelis's cozy, carpeted apartment, bathed in the luxuries afforded to a German lawyer, could never compensate for the coldness of her heart. Even the privacy of my own room and a maid at my disposal couldn't fill the ache in my heart for warmth and affection, which were absolutely missing in the sterile atmosphere of her Berlin home. Mrs. Michaelis compensated for her lonely, unhappy life by indulging herself in the few luxuries she could still find in Nazi Germany. She hired a tailor, who spent all day sewing and altering her wardrobe. The tailor was kept frantically busy, for Mrs. Michaelis's huge figure kept expanding each week as she ate to soothe her loneliness.

A cold and devious woman, she paraded a pompous Christianity. Her obesity distorted her face and added ten years to her actual age of forty-five. She never laughed or smiled, and I was certain she wanted me around only so she could inflict her aggressions on someone. In her stern, authoritative manner, she virtually growled at me when I made the least request. In a short time, I saw that I was a terrible inconvenience to her but that she would probably keep me as a virtual prisoner and obtain some diabolical delight from it. It seemed that all of Nazi Germany had gone mad. Life's absurdities and inconveniences were making many minds snap. But my education meant so much to me; enduring life with Mrs. Michaelis enabled me to attend a good Berlin school. I prayed day and night that Mrs. Michaelis would begin to act like the good Christian she claimed to be.

From my first day with her, I saw that my rations would be little better than what I'd had in Breslau. The maid sent me off to school each morning with only a cucumber sandwich. I was smart enough to realize that Mrs. Michaelis was using my ration card to get additional food for herself. I never even tasted most of the food that was supposed to be mine. My small meat rations were given to her tailor.

A Ration Card. *Courtesy United States Holocaust Memorial Museum*

The ever-present miracle in my life was God's hand of protection and provision for me. I met another Christian friend, Ruth Conrad, at school. Ruth frequently shared her family's rations with me. But since they hardly had enough for themselves, the morsels of food she brought couldn't ward off my impending malnutrition.

Mrs. Michaelis's promises of sending me home frequently to visit Mother also didn't materialize. Though my heart physically ached to go home, I thought perhaps it was just as well that I didn't, for Mother would worry about me if she knew about my ordeal in Berlin. I wrote her positive letters so she wouldn't have the added burden of worrying about me. In return, I lived for her letters that told me how she was reading her Bible and considering the claims of Jesus. With news like that, I felt sure I could endure almost anything.

God graciously blessed me that spring with a Nazi teacher who dared to like me. Actually, she was a member of the Nazi Party only because all PhDs were required to join—window dressing for the party. Although Dr. Streit had no faith in a personal God, she listened politely as I witnessed to the strength that Jesus gave me.

I trembled for a full day when I felt I must reveal my Jewish heritage to her. But as I awkwardly told her one day after school, she smiled faintly and simply replied, "I know, Anita, and it doesn't matter. I still want to be your friend."

It was just another sign to me that Jesus was in control of the chaos in Nazi Germany and in my life. It was as though God reaffirmed His special love for me by allowing me to have a teacher who liked me in spite of everything. She risked a great deal by being seen with me both after school as I walked her to the streetcar, and in the morning when I came to school early just to talk. We tended to avoid politics, and she was not overly interested in Christianity, so sometimes the talk was trivial. But it didn't matter. The important thing was that she listened to just about anything else I wanted to talk about, including all my silly, adolescent dreams that would never materialize in Nazi Germany.

By summer, the Führer had made himself the master of western Europe as he invaded Denmark, Norway, Belgium, Holland, Luxembourg, and France. They all would fall before the year's end. It began to look as though Italy would enter the war as an ally of Germany. But as long as England remained undefeated in the war, a complete German victory was not possible in the West. British resistance stiffened that spring and summer under the incomparable leadership of Winston Churchill. Britain was sending her planes in increasing numbers over the skies of Germany. As the Germans attacked Allied cities and sunk Allied ships, Britain began to retaliate by dropping bombs, and Germany started melting beneath her burning cities.

That August we heard terrifying news: The Germans had bombed a residential section of London, and word got out that the British Royal Air Force would retaliate by hitting Berlin. Thus, the war was brought home to Germany, and Berlin's air-raid shelters became my home away from home. If life for the German people had once been an inconvenience, it now was a hellish nightmare. The siege began in Berlin, but soon the whole country would be in rubble.

When the bombing began, we children thought of the nightly air raids as nothing more than dangerous thunderstorms, during which everyone scrambled for the shelters—only basements really. At first the British hit only government centers in Berlin. Sometimes, however, the shrill sirens interrupted our light sleep as often as three times a night. And each time we would dash frantically to the shelter beneath our apartment building.

The children smiled, knowing that more than one raid a night meant no school tomorrow. By 3:00 a.m., the bombing would end and we would return home. The next day we collected fragments of bombshells, making a game out of seeing who could find the most. Our homes and apartments weren't being torn apart yet, but our walls shook and the dust was raised.

Still, the raids took their toll. Germany was literally growing weary from the loss of sleep, and the shelters were damp and cold. As the war got worse, so did general living conditions. Yet no true German dared to let defeat or discouragement cross his mind. It was still unthinkable. What about the thousand-year Reich? Hitler surely had things under control; this was only a temporary inconvenience. It was a small price to pay for the Fatherland and the glorious days that lay ahead for the Reich.

I had hoped Mrs. Michaelis's church members would be an adequate substitute for the wonderful believers at St. Barbara's Lutheran Church in Breslau. Unfortunately, Mrs. Michaelis was representative of her church. Since my only experience with believers had been at Pastor Hornig's church, I assumed all Christians had the same loving spirit. But I was now being exposed to a phony brand of Christianity that allowed church members to gather socially and use the language of the pious Christian.

Finally, that summer, my ill-fed body began to rebel. Gazing into the tailor's full-length mirror, I saw vividly what my clothes had been telling me: I was growing dangerously thin, and my hair was gradually falling out because of malnutrition. Mrs. Michaelis passed it off nonchalantly, saying I was a fast-growing, gangly teenager. But the fact was I had been receiving only a third of the vitamins and calories I needed each day. My friend Ruth tried to compensate by bringing me more of her family's rations. She was risking a great deal by identifying herself openly as my friend, for she could be subjected to serious reprisals.

"I will not watch you starve to death," she insisted almost daily. "My family will simply do with less." My malnutrition would have occurred much sooner and would have been far more severe had it not been for the Conrads.

As Mrs. Michaelis decreased my rations, she increased her open hostility toward me. Early one morning she announced, "Anita, I want you to deny yourself all earthly pleasures. I'm trying to teach you to do that, you know. In the end it will be good for you."

"But Mrs. Michaelis," I protested, "you don't have to teach me something I already know so much about. How can I be denied something I've never had? Because of Hitler, I've never known earthly pleasures."

"Well, I will continue to teach you self-denial," she said. "It's good for all of us."

"But you don't deny yourself things," I said.

"Of course I do! I want you to know that I feel terrible grief, Anita Dittman. It gnaws at me night and day. I am an Aryan, but I made the mistake of marrying a Jew, and I'll pay for it the rest of my life."

"I didn't choose my parents, Mrs. Michaelis, but I'll pay for my existence as long as I live in Germany," I replied.

As we talked, a flushed feeling came over me, and I recognized the symptoms of a fever. Lack of sleep, improper diet, and emotional strain had made me susceptible to a serious flu virus. Mrs. Michaelis sent me to bed, saying, "Stay in bed, Anita, with the light off. Don't come to the supper table. We don't want to catch your illness."

That week the maid simply pushed bowls of cereal through my bedroom door and then quickly closed it. "Call me when you're finished," she said. "Just put the dishes outside your door."

I nearly gagged at the overdose of cold cereal in lukewarm milk every day. Even with Jesus as close to me as I knew He was, at times I felt terribly alone and abandoned. I needed Mother. When I was sick, she would bring me some pencils and paper so I could draw. She would check on me often and put her cool hand on my forehead. I hungered for emotional warmth far more than for food, and for several hours I was sure God had left me for another battlefront.

My food rations continued to dwindle, so I finally spoke up in protest to Mrs. Michaelis.

"Are my starvation rations a part of your plan to teach me self-denial?" I asked her boldly. Her face grew red with anger and her eyes flashed bitterly at me. She was a churning volcano, embittered by an unsuccessful marriage and the loss of her sons.

"Anita Dittman, what do you think I am? Do you think I'm a charitable Christian who loves to help needy children, or am I a cold person who takes out her frustration on helpless children?"

"You are the latter," I said calmly.

She stared at me for several seconds, stunned by my candidness. Her facial muscles grew more tense. As she swelled with anger, her enlarged body strained the seams of her clothing.

"How dare you say such a thing!" she said, scowling at me. "You have one week to beg my forgiveness or else I will throw you out, you little brat. You'll have to go back to Breslau, where they pick up your kind every day by the hundreds. The excellent education I am giving you will end. One week; do you understand?"

Although my opinion had not changed, I did apologize and stayed in school.

The air attack intensified in the fall of 1940 as Berlin received the brunt of the Allied bombing. As the bombs fell closer and closer to home, the game of war wore off; the children's curiosity and fantasy about war were replaced with cries of fright and panic as bombs ripped through apartments and houses. The basement bomb shelters were almost useless against a direct hit, for a shell would race through ten stories to the basement, burying hundreds of victims. As Hitler intensified the fighting on the battlefront, the Allies intensified their reign of terror from the sky.

Some residents refused to go to the shelters because they considered them nothing but giant tombs. Instead they stayed in their homes and hid under flimsy household objects. Those on whom God had His hand often were miraculously protected amid the exploding debris and flames, but eventually half a million people would perish from the bombs dropped on Germany.

Life in the shelters was nerve-racking. We couldn't move for fear of using too much oxygen. Even if bombs exploded all around us, we were careful not to utter an anti-Nazi statement because several staunch Nazis were sure to be in any given bomb shelter.

I lived for letters from Mother to tell me that she, Aunt Friede, and Aunt Elsbeth were all right. Another sister, Aunt Käte, had moved into the apartment, and I could almost hear those three nervous, self-centered sisters cackling at one another. They were impatient and intolerant of each other and especially criticized Mother's interest in Christ. By now I had decided that the enticement of a good education couldn't keep me in Berlin. I was even willing to endure the horrible bedbugs if I could have the love of Mother and Pastor Hornig and escape from Berlin's merciless air raids.

As the winter winds began to blow, I missed Mother and the familiarities of home even more. Christmas was in the air, and though Mrs. Michaelis assured me she would send me home for the holiday, I knew that at a moment's whim she could change her mind.

Then early in December, my school principal handed me a note: "Because of your non-Aryan background, you will no longer be allowed to attend classes at this school."

"Jesus, what have I done wrong that You deny me everything?" I pleaded as I walked home that afternoon. I couldn't even find Ruth Conrad or Dr. Streit to receive some comfort from them. It seemed that I would have to bear it all alone. My eyes watered from both the cold wind and the disappointment; my cheeks stung with tears that nearly turned to ice. I decided to call Pastor Hornig and pour out my troubles to him, assured that he wouldn't tell Mother and worry her.

Mrs. Michaelis wasn't at home when I arrived at the apartment. With my coat still on and the note clutched in my hand, I called St. Barbara's church, hoping to find Pastor Hornig there. The emotional dam within me was ready to burst. At thirteen and a half, I was trying to sort through the confusion of life in Germany as well as the turmoil of my own adolescence. I needed a sympathetic Christian adult to interpret the longings of my heart.

The phone rang several times before it was answered by the familiar voice of the one man on earth who genuinely cared for me. Upon hearing his kind voice, the dam burst.

"I want to come home!" I blurted out as tears rolled down my cheeks. "Pastor Hornig, help me come home."

"Anita, is that you?"

"Yes, and I don't care about school or anything except being with Mother! She is all I have in this mixed-up world. We need each other."

"What has happened? Why are you crying?"

"I can't go back to school here," I replied. "They gave me a note today that told me not to return because I'm not an Aryan."

"I'm sorry, Anita. I'm so sorry. But everyone in Germany is suffering, not just you. The Christians suffer, the Jews suffer, and even the Nazi sympathizers suffer."

"Pastor Hornig, Mrs. Michaelis has been cruel. My friend Ruth Conrad says I am suffering from malnutrition, because I'm always tired and weak and my hair keeps falling out."

"Why didn't you say something sooner?" Pastor Hornig asked, sounding alarmed. "I could have stepped in, Anita, and done something about that."

"Because I didn't want Mother to worry about me. She has enough to handle taking care of her sisters. But she will be upset when she sees me, because I've lost a lot of weight. You'd better break it to her."

"Anita, pack your things and come home. Have Mrs. Michaelis take you to the train depot tonight. Tell her the church will pay for your train ticket home. I think I know someone in our church who will help you with your school expenses here in Breslau. Besides, Breslau isn't being hit from the air; I've wanted you to leave Berlin for that reason. I will meet you tonight, Anita, at the train. Don't worry; do you hear? Everything will work out. We love you and would do anything for you."

I heard the magic words: "Come home!" The nightmare of the last several months vanished into insignificance with the thought of returning home and being there in time for Christmas! Bedbugs didn't matter. Crotchety Aunt Käte didn't matter. Even if I had to wear the yellow Star of David that would brand me as a Jew and put me into a class of people lower than a convict, that didn't matter either. If the Allies dropped bombs on Breslau, at least Mother and I would be together. If I never went beyond the seventh grade, I didn't care.

All that mattered was life and time spent with loved ones. How grateful I was to God for reaching down and loving me through the compassion of Mother and Pastor Hornig.

5

"OPEN UP!"

It was hard to get my strength back even though I was living at home again. Food rations decreased almost weekly, until we ate only one meal a day. Everyone had to tighten his belt because so much food was being sent to the German soldiers on the front lines.

Brown-shirted storm troopers were marching through the towns, terrorizing everyone and delighting in making life miserable for the Jews, whether by teasing and taunting or by acts of brutality. They ridiculed and beat Jews everywhere and randomly hauled off individuals or families to prison. Cattle cars were filled daily as trainloads of frightened Jews were shipped to secret destinations throughout the tranquil German countryside.

Pastor Hornig said that some anonymous church member had paid for all my classes and books at the König-Wilhelm Gymnasium* in Breslau. However, Mother and I were sure that it was the Hornigs themselves who had made the financial sacrifice. The tension was thick both at school and at home, for my three aunts bickered endlessly with one another.

---

* Secondary school for students preparing to enter university.

As I walked to the gymnasium, I saw bold signs proclaiming, "No Jews Allowed" on nearly every store. Other signs warned Germans to stay away from Jews, who had been banned from theaters, parks, and all recreational areas. Everywhere I looked, I saw anti-Jewish slogans and posters. Many of the posters had the photograph of a Jew who had just been arrested for some concocted crime. In sharp contrast, flashing neon signs illuminated Hitler's picture.

The Nazi flag was hung proudly outside of most homes in Breslau. Inside, Germans were required to have a picture of the Führer somewhere in the house. Hitler was pressing the Christian pastors to have his picture placed at the front of church altars.

With so many German men on the battlefield, the women had taken over their jobs. The streets were strangely empty of most automobiles, for they all were being used for military purposes. As a result, streetcars were as packed as the railroad cars to concentration camps.

Hitler's contorted and strained voice blasted hate propaganda from the radio almost daily; he frantically blamed "international financial Jewry" for the war and warned Germans that every living Jew was an archenemy of the Reich. Jews had absolutely no rights and weren't entitled to own property.

More and more Jews trembled behind locked doors. We learned that a brother and a sister of Mother's had been picked up and taken to a camp. Another brother and his wife took their own lives rather than face a concentration camp ordeal. It was inevitable that the random confiscation of Jews should hit our house that winter.

Mother tried to be a peacemaker for her three quarreling sisters. However, when she attempted to help them, they would gang up on her because of her growing love for Jesus, who Pastor Hornig had told her was the Jewish Messiah. Mother could no longer deny the power of Christ in our lives. She had to talk about Him; it was a natural overflow of love. But her sisters insisted that it was Jesus' followers who had hounded the Jews since the first century. They

claimed the Nazis were all Christians on the basis of them being
Gentiles and having attended Catholic or Lutheran churches. Many
of those very churches had now sold out to the Führer, allowing his
picture to be on their church altars. It made no sense to my aunts to
worship Jesus, a phony dead man in whose name millions of Jews
had been persecuted, tortured, and killed.

"But those people aren't really Christians!" I insisted, not fully
grasping the accuracy of my statement. "They just give real Christians a bad name."

"Nonsense!" insisted Aunt Elsbeth. "All Gentiles are Christians."

They either couldn't or wouldn't understand. Nor would they
believe Pastor Hornig when he told us that numerous Christians all
over Europe were actually helping the Jews at the risk of their own
lives. Ultimately, many of the believers went into concentration
camps themselves just because they had aided a Jew somewhere
in the Nazi world.

"You and your mother are traitors to our people!" Aunt Friede
said at least once a day. "You should be ashamed of yourselves."

Finally Mother would be quiet, but every night her sisters saw
her open her New Testament and read some more. They paced and
muttered to themselves about the tragedy of their sister's "blindness."

Since we shared the kitchen with so many others, we usually
ate at about 9:00 p.m. As we sat down to our meal one night early
that spring, we heard an abrupt knock on our door. Then came the
familiar "Open up!" that we had heard several times in our building.
Two more forceful knocks followed.

Mother went to the door, resigned to opening it and facing the
Nazis. She looked into the cold eyes of two Gestapo agents, who
greeted her with the familiar "Heil Hitler!"

Mother didn't respond, but she opened the door to let them
in. My aunts and I sat frozen in our chairs as the two Gestapo men
marched in, proudly wearing their Nazi uniforms and swastikas.

"We are here to arrest Käte Suessman. Which one of you is she?"

"It is I," Aunt Käte replied. "What have I done?"

Relief and horror were written on Mother's face. At least they didn't want me or her other two sisters, who were in poor health.

"Does it matter what the reason is for a Jew's arrest?" the self-appointed Gestapo spokesman answered. "Jews need only exist; that is reason enough for their arrest. You have five minutes to fill one bag with things, and that is all. Hurry now."

I pushed aside my plate of lettuce. *Dear Jesus*, I pleaded silently, *Aunt Käte cannot handle prison life. Just take her swiftly, dear Jesus.* Then I remembered that Aunt Käte did not yet know Jesus, and conflicting thoughts swept over me.

"I insist that you tell me why she's being arrested," Mother said, "and why are you taking her instead of me?"

"I only pick you people up," the Gestapo agent replied coldly, his arms folded impatiently in front of him. "I just follow my orders. I don't ask questions, and neither should you. Your neighbors, the Ephraims, are also being taken today. You can check at the police station tomorrow; they might tell you where they have been sent."

Aunt Käte filled a brown bag with some small essentials and then bundled up to leave for her unknown destination. All the rest of us choked back our tears, although Aunt Käte was being very brave as she faced the ordeal. Lining up at the door, we each gave her a hug before the Gestapo agents pushed her out into the hall. Across from us, we saw the whole Ephraim family silently gathering a few belongings. It made no sense to us that some Jews were being picked up while others weren't. Some family members were taken while others were left behind, even though for all Jews the everyday life anywhere in Germany was like living in a prison. But the selection for arrests seemed to be done at random, perhaps on the whim of the Gestapo officer who was in charge for the day.

Aunt Käte was led down the stairs and put into a Gestapo

wagon while Aunt Friede, Aunt Elsbeth, Mother, and I gazed sadly out our front window at the agony below. Normally an extremely nervous lady, Aunt Käte was unbelievably brave. We stared blankly as the wagon drove off down the street and grew small in the distance. Finally the war and Hitler's personal vengeance against the Jewish people had visited my immediate family.

That month Bulgaria was peacefully occupied. Then Germany invaded Yugoslavia, and soon tanks would roll into Athens. Hitler gave an injunction demanding merciless harshness in the war. Whereas at one time the German code of ethics had protected civilians and property, now everyone and everything was to be destroyed by the German soldiers. But every such act of brutality only increased the Allied assault on Germany, so in the end every German paid for the Führer's madness.

All internal affairs were being handed over to Martin Bormann, who began to carry out a ruthless assault on the Christian churches in Germany. More than ever we feared for the Hornigs and the believers at our church, for they would be prime targets for Bormann's men because of their interest in and love for the Jewish people. Gestapo agents always were planted in the church services now.

The fresh breezes of spring 1941 brought us little relief from our agony. I gave serious thought to dropping out of school because of the rampant anti-Semitism at the gymnasium. My teachers followed Nazi orders to be hard on all students who weren't Aryans, and the other young people didn't want to risk being my friend. I felt terribly lonely there—for a fourteen-year-old without a friend is like a violin without a bow.

One by one the apartments in our Jewish tenement were emptying as the arrests increased. In June, we heard the dreaded knock again. This time they came for Aunt Friede, who was seventy-three. We tried very hard to swallow our tears again, for we knew it would only upset Aunt Friede more to see us crying over her. Again, no explanation was given and no destination revealed.

A great part of the terrifying fear related to the arrests was the unknown factor of the prisoner's destination. Was it jail or a concentration camp? Was it a work camp or a gas chamber or a firing squad? One seldom knew until sometimes family members received a postcard from prison or perhaps word was smuggled out that the person had been killed. The fate of millions would never be known. They would simply become statistics.

We sat quietly as Aunt Friede gathered a handful of belongings. Mother smiled bravely at me, trying to comfort me from across the room.

"She is a sick, old lady," Mother protested to the Gestapo agents. "It would be better for you to take me. I am strong and healthy."

"My orders are to pick up Friede Markuse," one of the men replied.

"I will be back in a week," Aunt Friede said stubbornly.

Suddenly bedbugs, crowded ghettos, and meager rations didn't matter at all. All that mattered was staying together, praying to God, and trusting that He had everything under control. My heart cried for the Jews who had no faith in God, their Deliverer. They would die shaking their fists at God or Jesus or anyone who happened to be there.

We kissed Aunt Friede and watched the old, white-haired lady hobble down the street on her arthritic feet. Balancing herself with her cane, she was helped into the police wagon—a pathetic and haunting sight that burned itself into my memory.

Two weeks later the ugly scene repeated as Aunt Elsbeth was picked up. The Gestapo virtually pushed our door down and then screamed at us.

"Which one of you is Elsbeth Suessman?"

Aunt Elsbeth's feeble heart nearly stopped beating as she was ordered to gather her things. Then the Gestapo agents labeled some of her few remaining possessions.

"These are now the property of the state," they said. "We will pick them up later. You are not to touch them; do you understand?"

"This woman has a bad heart," Mother said as they waited for Aunt Elsbeth. "She is under a doctor's care and must receive constant medical attention. Will she get that where you are taking her?"

"Shut up!" came the reply. Impatiently they paced the apartment as Aunt Elsbeth gathered her things.

"That's enough!" one said. "Come with us now!"

Aunt Elsbeth was white with fear, but resistance would do no good.

One by one or all at once, families disappeared and were separated in the ordeal of Nazi Germany in 1941. We never saw Aunt Käte, Aunt Friede, or Aunt Elsbeth again.

* * *

Hitler's hunger for power and blood had no end. Next he invaded Russia in an effort to eliminate the "Eastern menace" of Bolshevism. The Führer didn't realize, of course, that this was a fatal miscalculation. A world war was now inevitable. America pledged economic aid, and the Allies started fighting back even harder.

Hitler was sure the Russian campaign would be swift, a fair-weather war. Thus the Russian winter became as much his enemy as the Russian soldier. More than 750,000 German soldiers would die from the winter elements as they became bogged down in their advance on Moscow. Because of the devastating defeat, the Jews would suffer even more and be made to pay for Hitler's mistake.

In that summer of 1941, Mother and I grew even closer as our safety grew yet more precarious. At least once a day we remarked how glad we were that Hella had gotten to England safely before the war began. Almost all of our friends had been arrested, although the Sandbergs were still in our building and Mother's two Hebrew Christian friends, Mrs. Czech and Mrs. Wolf, remained free.

Off and on Mother returned to forced labor, usually doing a man's heavy work to earn her pitifully small amount of welfare money. We tenderly savored the time we had together, dreaming of and imagining better days when we could return to the weekly church activities. We looked ahead longingly to the time when Mother would play with her grandchildren or even marry again.

"Mother, there's no terror like that which comes out of the sky in the middle of the night," I said as we sipped tea one cool summer evening. In Berlin the roar of an engine meant a plane would drop its bombs on us. It was fun at first; we made a game of it, and we knew we probably could skip school the next day. But then plaster began to fall into the shelters, and bomb fragments came in. Finally, the bombs exploded in some of the shelters, but they always missed mine, even though several buildings were leveled just a block away. "God must look favorably on Breslau. Mother, do you have any doubt that Jesus has been protecting you and me?"

"None at all," she answered pensively. "It was very difficult sorting through my feelings when Friede, Käte, and Elsbeth were here, but Jesus knows I don't have to give Him a parade and that I can express my appreciation silently and inwardly. You still have a child's exuberance, Anita. You are so expressive and so filled with hope. Don't lose it, even when things get worse."

"When will they?"

"I don't know, Anita, but I think Hitler made a mistake by declaring war on Russia. Someday the Americans will enter the war, and then Germany will be finished—but not before she gets what she deserves for the pain she creates for Europe. Pastor Hornig said God would judge her for her terrible treatment of the Jews, because the Bible says that will always happen to those who mistreat God's people. I believe it. But, for the madness of the guilty the innocent also suffer.

"Just so we can be together." It was my sustaining hope.

"That we cannot be sure of. Every day families are separated;

there is no pattern to the arrests, you know."

Mother paused a moment and then she said, "Anita, I have heard from your father. He is sorry for the way things have turned out. He gave me his telephone number, just in case there is anything he can do if you or I get arrested. I do not think he tries to trick us, Anita. I think his sorrow is real for leaving us, and he may be able to help you if you should be left alone."

Bitterness ate at me like a cancer. Father could have prevented a lot of our hardship by sticking with us, yet the awful pressures put on him by the Nazis made it understandable that he had buckled under them and run for his life.

Reaching into her purse, Mother took out a piece of paper and handed it to me. "Your father is going to remarry soon, Anita. Here is the telephone number where you might reach him."

I reluctantly took the paper.

"I pray I will never have to use it," I said quietly.

That week a new family, Mr. and Mrs. Rosen and their son, Joachim, moved into the Ephraims' old apartment. Joachim was my age, and he and his parents were Orthodox Jews, just as the Sandbergs were.

Joachim quickly became a light in my life. We hovered between childhood and young adulthood; and though our games were often childish, our feelings for one another bordered on the adult level. At fourteen, we both struggled to leave our child worlds behind, yet it was only our fantasy world that made Nazi Germany tolerable. So we clung to childhood while at the same time we struggled to enter adulthood and understand what was happening to us.

I feared I would lose Joachim if I talked too much about Jesus; I bit my tongue every time I wanted to tell him about Christ. So many of my friends had come and gone. I didn't fit into either the Aryan or the Nazi world; and my Jewish friends who were not believers accepted me only up to a point. Then fear, mistrust, or prejudice would enter, thwarting any real friendship. I knew I possessed the capacity to be a good friend; I only wanted the chance to prove it.

I prayed that Jesus would understand my cowardice, but in place of His peace I felt a nagging, haunting tug at my heart that seemed to say I must forsake everyone—even Mother—if I was to follow Him. Bible lessons I had learned from Pastor Hornig confirmed that. Christ would never permit me to place Him second or third in my life.

Joachim knew I believed in Jesus, but as long as I didn't talk about it, he didn't mind. He was sure it was a passing fantasy and that the war would convince me that the Messiah could not have come yet.

"If Jesus is the Messiah," Joachim said one summer afternoon, "where is the peace He is supposed to bring? The whole world is engulfed in war. Your Jesus was an imposter. Besides, it's ridiculous to say that God would have a son." And with a shaking, angry voice, Joachim tried to change the subject.

I took a hundred questions a week to Pastor Hornig, for I was attending confirmation classes at his home as often as I dared venture out into Breslau's chaotic streets. After class, I always managed to linger as long as I could to ask him for answers to some of Joachim's questions.

"The peace the Messiah brings," Pastor Hornig explained, "may be a peace that is within the heart. But the Bible says that someday Jesus will establish His kingdom on the earth, and then there will be literal peace, and the lion will lie down by the lamb. At that time Jesus will sit on the throne of David in Jerusalem, and the whole nation of Israel will acknowledge Him as the Savior and Messiah! What a glorious day that will be!"

"It's difficult for me to keep my faith hidden in my heart," I said to the pastor.

"But too many believers make the mistake of talking too much about Christ to their Jewish friends," he answered. "Sometimes we must win them to Jesus simply by loving them and by praying for them, Anita. We must let God impress on them their need for Christ and not ramble on about our faith if it offends them. When they see that our lives are significantly different, they will begin to ask questions. It will be like that with Joachim. I believe that is why you have been left in Germany, Anita, so you can be an effective witness by your life. Hella could not. You must show others that you have God's peace when the world around us goes to pieces. Don't ever let Satan take away your peace and joy. Remember that you are Satan's special target because you can bring hope to God's own people. I am convinced that both you and your mother will influence many Jews before the war is over. Every day my hope dims a little more for getting the two of you out of Germany. God seems to be impressing me with the fact that you and your mother must remain and be witnesses here."

Pastor Hornig's words about our staying in Germany confirmed the feeling in my own heart.

"Why is it the Jewish people seem to suffer the most?" I asked. "Is it because we killed Jesus?"

"Our sin killed Jesus, Anita! It was all part of God's plan of salvation that Jesus die for our sins. Besides, the Romans could have stopped the crucifixion, but they didn't. They let an innocent man die, and they knew it."

Joachim and I spent the waning weeks of summer together. We knew that even darker days lay ahead, for I would soon return to the gymnasium and he to his all-Jewish school. The tenement baked in the August sun, and our playground was often the dirty halls or smelly basement of our building. Joachim's faded yellow Star of David instantly branded him as a Jew wherever he went, so he usually chose to stay indoors.

"We will always be friends," Joachim told me one day as we sat on the front steps of our building. "When the war is over, I want to take you to the theater and other nice places. If we ever get separated, will you promise to write me?"

"I promise," I said, "but we need to pray that the war ends before we are separated. Look at our empty ghetto," I continued, pointing to the deserted streets. "Almost everyone is gone."

How I wanted Joachim to know that we worshiped the same God and hoped in the same Messiah! We were so close in our beliefs and yet so far away.

But life in the steaming ghetto was bearable as long as I had Mother and now Joachim. At night when I put my head on my pillow, an unexplainable peace came over me. Perhaps it was just a secure feeling because I was loved by Mother, Pastor Hornig, the believers at the church, and Joachim. Whatever it was, I felt sure God was giving it to me as a special gift. It was His way of compensating for my life in Germany under Hitler. Perhaps it was God's still, small voice saying, "I love you, Anita Dittman, and I am demonstrating My love by sending people to you who love you very much. Even if you are left alone, I will show My love for you in special ways, for I will never leave you."

With that quiet assurance, I would fall asleep and rest peacefully, even with the strange conviction that darker days lay ahead for Germany—and for Mother and me.

Life at the gymnasium was bearable only because my nineteen-year-old teacher, Helga Fritsch, secretly hated the Nazis and chose not to persecute me. In fact, she even took the risk of inviting me to a party at her home during the fall of 1941. I saw it as another manifestation of God's goodness to me amid life's turmoil.

Pastor Hornig continued to make sure that I had enough money to buy the expensive schoolbooks and keep up my tuition payments. I was even more convinced that the money came directly from his family.

Mother frequently arrived home well after dark from laboring on her assigned jobs. Often her earnings were just pennies an hour. It was hard for me to come home to a dark, empty apartment, but perhaps God was preparing me for long, lonely days ahead.

As fall turned into early winter, two startling events occurred: Pearl Harbor was attacked and Hitler declared war on the United States. Mother's expression as she came home on the night when we heard the news revealed to me the seriousness of the situation. Just as Mother predicted, America would enter the war and Germany would really be finished. It was no longer a European war; it had become a world war. But every day that the battlefront got a little hotter for the German soldier, the persecution got more severe for the Jew.

"Joachim," I exclaimed as we met in the hall that night, "have you heard the news? America is entering the war."

"Maybe they will bring it to an end," he said optimistically. "Perhaps it's a blessing in disguise for us. Do you suppose so?"

But two days later, early in the morning before I left for school, the Gestapo marched into our building once again. We could hear their shiny Nazi boots stomping defiantly upstairs. As they walked down the long hall, all the residents shuddered in their rooms, each waiting for that fateful knock on the door. When the heavy footsteps marched past a room, the occupants breathed a sigh of relief but grieved for those who would hear the knock. Today the Nazis pounded on the Rosens' door.

"Open up!" I heard the Gestapo agents yell. I didn't dare open our door, but I glued my ear to the door to listen.

I heard the Gestapo men push their way into the Rosens' apartment across the hall. "You have five minutes to gather your things," came the familiar command. "The three of you will come with us to the synagogue. You each may fill one bag with possessions. Don't ask questions; just do as you are told, and it will be to your advantage."

Anita with two of her friends from school. Anita is on the right—14-1/2 years old—1941.

"Mother," I whispered loudly as tears filled my eyes, "Joachim is being taken with the Rosens!"

"You knew it would happen, Anita."

I agonized because I hadn't been able to share Christ with him, blaming myself for my unbelievable cowardice. No matter what Pastor Hornig had said about sharing Christ with our lives more than our words, it had been inexcusable of me not to try to make Joachim a believer.

"They're being taken to the synagogue," I said to Mother, who was getting ready for work. "I will visit him tonight, Mother. I must say good-bye to him."

Only one synagogue was left in Breslau after the burnings of 1938 and 1939. Recently it had been made into a prison for Jews who were waiting for processing before being sent off to the camps.

I could almost see Mother's thoughts written across her face. She had even formulated the words in her mind to insist that I not visit Joachim; but as she saw the tears run down my cheeks, she kept silent. In the end, she thought my fighting endurance would be my salvation. Why should she try to squelch it?

"Your furniture now belongs to the state," I heard one of the Gestapo men say to the Rosens.

I knew Joachim wanted to come and say good-bye but that it was impossible. The Gestapo had no time for silly sentimentality or young love. Arrests were a hurry-up-and-wait scene when Jews were hauled off to the processing centers, where they sometimes sat for days until they were deported to Bergen-Belsen, Treblinka, Dachau, Auschwitz, Theresienstadt, and other infamous camps.

The Rosens hardly said a word as they gathered their things.

Finally I heard their door close and all of them march down the hall. Running to the front window, I peeked out and watched them climb into the back of a snow-covered police wagon. Joachim didn't even look up my way, but I knew he didn't want to give me away or even admit to our friendship for fear it would endanger me more. My eyes followed that familiar police wagon as it disappeared down the street again, leaving only a trail of vapor in the cold morning air.

After school that day, I made my way to the crumbling synagogue.

During the long walk in the December cold, I considered the paradox of Nazi Germany. As Christmas approached, Germans celebrated the birth of Jesus; yet they worshiped the godless Nazis. The peace, joy, love, and hope that are synonymous with Christmas were strangely muted in Hitler's Germany, but few gave up the futile dream of the marvelous thousand-year Reich. Few were ready to allow the idea of defeat to enter their minds, even though smoke from burning Berlin rose five miles high in the sky and uncounted thousands of German soldiers were dying on the Russian battlefront.

Routinely the Russians announced the names of their captured German prisoners over the airwaves of underground radio stations. The prisoners' relatives knew they would never see their husbands or brothers again when they heard their names; the camps in Siberia never sent anyone home.

I wrapped my scarf around my face as the bitter-cold wind stung me. My fingers felt frozen, but it was a small price to pay to see Joachim just once more. I walked for nearly an hour before the synagogue came into view. I saw a hastily built fence around the structure, with a number of Gestapo and SS men standing guard.

Please, dear Jesus, allow me to go inside and see Joachim one more time, I prayed as I neared the building. *I'll tell him about You this time. Maybe he's so scared he will listen now.*

I stood for several long moments outside the gate leading to the synagogue, for once wanting to be noticed by the Gestapo so that I wouldn't have to call to them. As they chatted among themselves and moved frequently in and out of the building, I could hear them laughing and making jokes about the "pitiful specimens of humanity" that sat trapped inside the synagogue walls. Finally, one guard spotted me.

"What do you want, kid?" he shouted as I leaned on the entrance gate.

"I want to see my friend, Joachim Rosen. I have a very important message for him. It will take only a minute."

He strolled toward me with a smirk on his face, "Where he's going, it doesn't matter if he gets your message." He balanced his rifle as though he were on the battlefront.

"Sir, you can be with me when I give him the message," I said politely.

The guard looked at me through the bars of the gate for several long seconds. Since I still wasn't wearing the Star of David and because my hair had Aryan blond streaks, he obviously didn't recognize my Jewish heritage.

"What is the message? Give it to me, and I will determine if it is important or not."

"I just want to tell him that I love him," I said.

"Why would a pretty girl like you want to love a Jew?" he said angrily. "Don't you know it is a sin against the Reich to be a Jew-lover?"

My honesty had nearly gotten me into trouble. Germans could be shot on sight if they sympathized with the Jews.

"Well, hurry up about it!" he commanded as he opened the gate. "I will give you exactly three minutes to deliver your silly message, and then I will drag you out."

I ran past the guards, into the dimly lit synagogue. As I entered the front door, I stopped abruptly, hit by an air of despair. Hundreds of Jews sat on the straw-covered synagogue floor, while a dozen small children and babies cried because of the cold and confusion. Some people chatted with family or friends to ease their tension, but most stared blankly ahead. At least these prisoners had been taken as families, and they would probably be sent to prison together. Even the bearded old men and weary old women sat on the floor, resigned to their ominous fate.

By the time I saw the Rosens sitting together in a corner, I knew my three minutes were rapidly ticking away. Finally, Joachim spotted me in the doorway, and we ran toward each other and embraced.

"What are you doing here, Anita?" Joachim scolded. "How did you get in? Don't you know how dangerous this is?"

"I don't care. I just had to say good-bye. Jesus has assured me that He will protect you, Joachim! Maybe we could meet here in Breslau when the war is over."

"Sure, but you get out of here now, Anita! They could close the door and lock you in here, too. It would save them a trip to your apartment." He put his arm around me and kissed me on the cheek.

"I love you, Anita. We'll meet after the war is over. I'll find you somehow. Go now."

"Joachim, Jesus loves you very much. I do, too."

He pushed me away as the Gestapo guard came toward me, took me by the arm, and escorted me out of the synagogue and to the front gate. As we reached the gate, he opened it and pushed me outside.

"Beat it, kid. By rights, I should turn you in; but since it's almost Christmas, I won't. Go home."

Thank You, Jesus, I prayed silently.

As I headed home against the strong wind, I thought of the wonderful months Joachim and I had together as friends. He would always have a special place in my heart. A strange sense of peace about him came over me and would always remain, even though I would never see him again.

6

forced Labor

Hitler's attention was focused mainly on the Russian front in the spring of 1942, though the Africa corps drove farther and farther east toward the British-held Middle East. The Americans joined England's Royal Air Force in dropping bombs on German cities. In the coming weeks and months, Cologne, Rostock, Lubeck, and Berlin would become piles of rubble. But, thankfully, the planes still avoided Breslau.

That spring brought both the bitter and the sweet. Our good friends the Sandbergs were finally taken away. We sorrowed as we remembered the longing of their hearts to be reunited with their sons, who had fled to England before the war.

That May I turned fifteen, and I finished my confirmation classes with Pastor Hornig. Mother scraped a few cents together to make me a lovely white dress. Pastor Hornig tested me in front of the entire congregation at St. Barbara's; it was one of the highlights of my life. I was thrilled to be able to please Pastor Hornig and Mother as I gave all the right answers in my test. Mother looked at me proudly from the audience. My eyes flashed between Pastor Hornig and Mother as I drank in their looks of approval and praise. This was the best gift I could give them. My eyes also saw an unfamiliar face in the congregation. We learned later that it was another

Nazi spy. It was no secret to anyone in Breslau that Pastor Hornig aided Jews—both believers and unbelievers. Gestapo agents followed him frequently and planted themselves in the church services, to monitor any anti-Nazi statements.

Shortly after my confirmation, I was handed another familiar note in school, telling me not to return to classes because of my Jewish heritage.

That same week, the Gestapo sent a notice to Mother, ordering her to report to a canning factory for heavy labor. She would be paid the equivalent of twenty cents an hour for peeling onions by hand, running a cabbage-shredding machine, and lifting heavy boxes for ten hours a day. At first she worked the night shift, from 10:00 p.m. until 8:00 a.m. I always had a small meal ready for her when she returned in the morning, her eyes red and swollen from peeling onions, and her back throbbing from lifting boxes.

About the same time that spring, Reinhard Heydrich died. He was one-third of the Eichmann-Himmler-Heydrich trio—the masterminds behind the Jewish persecution. The blood of thousands—perhaps millions—of Jews was on his hands.

By early summer, the Führer was the undisputed master of Europe, from the Volga to the English Channel. He also had broken Egypt and was making significant gains in Russia. The Russian invasion, however, would stop at Stalingrad.

Mother and I continued to thank God every day for our glorious freedom. By the rest of the world's standards, we were pitifully persecuted and deprived; by German standards, we were wonderfully free and wealthy. City after city boasted that it was free of all Jews, yet Mother and I had life, each other, the church, and, most of all, the love and protection of Jesus. Though some of our luxuries could be abruptly stopped, we were savoring them while they lasted. At the same time, summer days were long and lonely for me as Mother slept and then left for work in the evening. It was a risk to be outdoors much, and the Christian young people from the church dared not come into the Jewish ghetto and identify themselves as obvious sympathizers. My Jewish friends and playmates were all gone. An eerie atmosphere hung over the streets of Breslau. Perhaps it was felt all over Germany. It was as though actual demons from hell gleefully danced in the air over the country. Sometimes I felt as if God had grieved so much over man's hatred and prejudice that He had abandoned Germany for a season. Perhaps He looked down at Germany as He'd once looked down on His Son's crucifixion; He let evil take its course.

It was a paradox: Just as I felt the most isolated, God would manifest His power and control over all our circumstances. His watchful care and protection during the war over those of us who believed on the name of Jesus could fill hundreds of volumes. His protection of Mother and me was just a tiny particle of sand on the giant seashore of His safety and love.

I almost felt happy when the Gestapo ordered me to report to the canning factory for forced labor in the fall of 1942. Both Mother and I would be working the day shift, and we thanked God that we could again spend our time together. We worked six days a week for ten hours a day, still earning the same small wage. Our day began before 5:30 a.m. with a long streetcar ride through deserted Breslau. Then we had about a ten-block walk to the factory, where our workday started at 7:00 a.m.

The work was tedious, for Mother and I shredded onions and peeled carrots all day long. The sulfur in the onions made our skin turn black, and our eyes always stung. However, the onion fumes were so strong that our supervisor stayed away from us, and we were left alone to visit together. We prayed and talked and dreamed of better days ahead, occasionally eating an onion when the hunger pains got too severe.

Because I was young and strong, I was often told to do heavy labor in other departments of the factory. I might haul one-hundred-pound bags of apples, which also allowed me the pleasure of sneaking an apple or two for my lunch. The red, juicy apples were worth more than gold to hungry Germans.

Most of the factory's employees were Jewish women, the last Jews in Breslau. A few were Jewish Christians like us, and that is why they still had their "freedom." Some of them had been won to Christ through Pastor Hornig. However, many of the workers were Jewish unbelievers who were simply marking time before they would be taken away. Almost every day another Jewish employee didn't return to the factory, and we knew what had happened.

A few unbelievers listened politely as Mother and I spoke of Jesus, the Jewish Messiah. Most of them, however, had lost any remnants of whatever faith they might have had; they had seen simply too much hatred and heartache to believe that God would allow it.

"Either God is love or God doesn't exist," one Jewish lady insisted. "It is obvious that no God of love would permit what is happening. Therefore, He is just refuge for the neurotic, the fearful, and the lonely."

To this day, the Nazi Holocaust continues to prevent many Jewish people from believing in God. Satan uses it as the biggest stumbling block for the numerous Jews who can't accept that a loving, all-powerful God would allow such a horrible thing to happen. Granted, millions perished, yet God also allowed millions to survive. With the onslaught of winter, we had to contend with the awful cold. The area of the factory in which we worked was barely heated, and each morning the streetcar was so crowded that we had to ride on the exposed upper deck. We became thoroughly frozen before starting our long workday. I stuffed my shoes with newspapers to add some insulation; nevertheless, my body seldom thawed out before early the next morning, and then I had to go out and do it all over again.

A portion of every evening was spent standing in line for our pitiful rations. Lines were long and the people impatient and pushy. It made no difference if one was a Jew, Christian, Nazi, or atheist—we all had to stand in line, and we all suffered from the lack of proper food and vitamins. Still, no one in line dared complain, though some were secretly questioning the Führer now. As Germans received word of more and more of their loved ones being killed in flaming cities and on the battlefront, their loyalty to the Reich began to falter.

That winter we were required to work on Sundays, so we lost our precious day of worship at church. Life became only work and sleep and monotony and fear, except for the wonderful moments spent praying or encouraging a faltering believer. Mother and I stood side by side at work and prayed for Hella, the Sandbergs, the Rosens, Aunt Friede, Aunt Elsbeth, and Aunt Käte, and even for Father. We also prayed for Mother's other relatives, whose whereabouts and status we didn't know. For ourselves, we prayed that God would continue to be merciful, for we still hadn't heard the dreaded Gestapo knock for us.

And we thanked God! Although the Allied planes darkened the skies over Germany like bands of locusts, they still had not bombed Breslau. We also thanked God for the Allies' increased victories and their sudden show of strength in Africa, Russia, and Europe.

In December, I was transferred to the factory's front office to do filing, operate the switchboard, and help with other routine office duties. Though I hated to be separated from Mother, at least the office was heated and I could do sit-down work. Our boss seemed to like me, but I was suspicious of his motives. Since most of the office workers were Germans, I wondered what fellowship I could possibly have with them. Perhaps it would be better to shiver in misery with like-minded people.

On the first day of my new job, I saw that I would be required to eat lunch with the German workers rather than with my Jewish friends. But when the lunch whistle blew, I walked defiantly past the German lunchroom and headed for the Jewish lunchroom. My boss, amazed at my stubbornness, shouted at me as I walked away from him and his prejudiced coworkers.

"Anita! Where do you think you are going?"

"To be with Mother and my friends, sir," I replied as I turned around.

"I forbid it!" he said. "You belong here with us."

"Sir, those Jews are my relatives," I answered. "If I cannot eat with them, then I request that you transfer me back to factory work. I do not want your comfortable office work if I must forsake those people."

My boss slammed his fist down on a table, and everyone stopped what he or she was doing. "I will report you to the Gestapo!" he insisted.

"Please do so, Mr. Goerlitz," I said calmly. "May I report back to the factory work, then?"

When he saw that I wouldn't back down, his expression softened. "I need you in the office, Anita. Please reconsider and stay away from the Jews."

"Never, Mr. Goerlitz. Never. They are my people."

I turned and walked toward the Jewish lunchroom. Mr. Goerlitz didn't bother me then or in the coming weeks, even though I continued to work in the office. Nor did he report me to the Gestapo. In fact, he treated me with newfound respect and admiration because I was willing to give up the comforts of office work to do heavy labor with the Jews.

"Anita!" Mother scolded when I related the incident to her. "You must *not* talk back to the Nazis. You and I are living on borrowed time. We must not hurry our arrest."

"I will before I'll deny you and the others," I said. "I can tell by the way Mr. Goerlitz looks at me that he wants me to be more than an office worker. I would rather die than let him think for one moment that I am interested in him or his Nazi party."

"You be careful and don't push him," Mother said. "Be politely cool to him and stall for time."

But Mr. Goerlitz never challenged me again as I passed by the German eating area at noon. An old German saying goes, "The coward is despised both by friend and foe, but the brave is admired even by his enemies." Perhaps it had proved true in my case.

* * *

The Reich suffered a terrible defeat at Stalingrad as the Russians captured 220,000 German prisoners in February 1943. Solemn music was played for three days on the radio as all Germans mourned the loss. At last, Germany was experiencing the type of pain she had been inflicting on others.

We had heard that defeat was also occurring in North Africa, and the air war against Germany was merciless now. A layer of smoke blanketed the land as Hamburg and other cities were being hit day and night. A concentrated Allied attack on German U-boats caused the Germans to lose the battle in the Atlantic.

Finally, the Allies demanded the unconditional surrender of the Reich, but for Hitler that was unthinkable. Instead, he declared that an attitude of defeatism would be punishable by death, and the empty propaganda that promised a glorious day for Germany continued to be screamed over the airwaves.

Calling the Russians "subhumans," Hitler promised their eventual defeat and told his soldiers that a Russian life was worthless. All efforts had to be poured into the defeat of Russia, he said, without any care for life. His proclamation included the deaths, if necessary, of innocent women and children.

How much longer would the German people believe in the illusion of the glorious Fatherland? How much longer would they follow the mad pied piper and trust him with their sons, fathers, and husbands, many of whom would never leave the Siberian prisoner-of-war camps? How much longer would they be blindly obedient to the Führer, who admittedly had no compassionate thought for a human life? He even willingly sacrificed his own German people if they weren't perfect specimens of the Aryan race. When would the prayers of Christians around the world hasten the demise of the German demagogue and strangle Satan's attempt to bring only sorrow and sighing into the world? *How much longer, God?* We knew that one swift blow of God's judgment could end the despair, and we believed that real Christians around the world surely had calluses on their knees from praying for the nightmare to end.

But the Germans continued to dig out their cities and tighten their belts and sing the songs of the Reich, even while the names of ninety-thousand German prisoners of war were broadcast into their homes from Russia.

Mother and I were transferred that winter to the Oberhammer Wine Bottling Company, where again we worked side by side at heavy, forced labor with a handful of Breslau's remaining Jews. More Jewish believers were working there than at the other factory, so we were able to enjoy some days of good fellowship when our supervisor wasn't present.

From 7:00 a.m. until 5:00 p.m., we rinsed empty wine bottles before loading them into huge carriers twice the size of a coffin. Then two of us women would haul the carriers several yards to an elevator, from where the bottles would go on to the next process and finally be filled again with wine. Since we no longer had the built-in safety device of onion fumes, we had to guard our conversation in case our supervisor was listening. But whenever he stepped out of our area, we chatted away furiously, as though that conversation might be our last. "It is a miracle," I whispered to Mother, "that God keeps our strength up with so little food."

I looked at Mother, who was thin from the forced labor and growing old before her time. Still, her spirits had not diminished, and she was a spiritual strength to some of the other factory women. She never showed bitterness toward the Nazis; I always marveled at the way God took away any bitterness and anger.

16 years old

"God will use the Allies to deliver us soon, Anita," Mother said. "But we must pray that it is before 'the final solution' becomes final." She was referring to Hitler's command to find a final solution to the Jewish problem.

I longed to continue my education. I had dreams of going into chemistry or of working with small children, but all my hopes would be thwarted if I could not finish school. Germany wasn't kind to her uneducated, and although Mother and I still dreamed of going to England to be with Hella, I knew England would not look favorably on me either if I were an unskilled laborer. As I pictured myself doing manual labor similar to my factory work for the rest of my life, somehow that fate seemed worse than living under the Nazis forever. Within myself, I felt a wealth of creativity that needed training and channeling. I longed to make even the smallest contribution to humanity and to Christianity, but both desires seemed hopeless under the swastika. It was even more reason to pray that God would judge Germany and free her prisoners.

As winter turned into the spring of 1943, we heard that the Allies had won the war in Africa, which gave Mother and me a surge of hope. But true to the pattern, as the Reich suffered, our supervisor became more strict and rigid, allowing hardly any conversation during our long workday. Only hungry rats scurrying along the beams above us broke the monotony.

Mother and I developed a kind of sixth sense of communication. Working together daily now, we could communicate with facial gestures or with body language. We knew the war's turning tide just by feeling the tension in the air at the factory. Rumors began to fly about some of the Reich's concentration camps being liberated in the coming year. The camps now held millions of Jews from Germany, France, Belgium, Holland, Austria, Poland, Czechoslovakia, Hungary, and the Balkans.

However, our dreams were suddenly shattered one balmy

spring day when we heard about the destruction of the Warsaw ghetto. Five hundred thousand Jews had been herded into the ghetto to starve to death. Finally the Germans went in to kill them or crowd them into death camps; however, the starving but determined Jews fought back with everything they had. Then Hitler sent in three thousand more troops to quickly take over the ghetto with tanks, armored cars, artillery, and flamethrowers. Only five hundred Jews lived to tell of the annihilation of the ghetto and its people.

That week we could hardly speak to one another without choking back tears of grief and anger; even within the purest heart, bitterness raged toward the Nazis. Our faith was shaken and our hope dimmed. The atheists among us cursed, while the Jewish unbelievers withdrew into themselves. The religious Jews prayed harder and asked why. We Christians comforted one another and realized that some answers would be available only in heaven.

"It is not enough that we pray for the war to end, Anita," Mother said one evening. "We must pray that God will grant us safety while it is coming to a close. God will judge our country, and the innocent will suffer too. Anita, pray that God will encircle us with His marvelous love and protection even while the Allied assault rages all around us."

We greatly missed the spiritual food from the church and the blessed fellowship with the believers. St. Barbara's had been a true haven of rest.

"The spiritual isolation hurts me more than the physical deprivation," Mother confessed to me that same evening. "My body has adjusted to little food or rest, but it cannot adjust to the spiritual starvation."

As I listened to the ache in Mother's voice for the believers' fellowship and inspiration, I realized that she probably never would have grown so rapidly in her faith in Christ had it not been for the war and all its absurdities. God surely comforts the afflicted, but

7

JAUNDICE

early that summer I noticed I had some disturbing physical symptoms: constant fever, nausea, and extreme fatigue. I was dangerously thin again, and after ten hours of work and two hours in line for rations each day, I could barely make it home at night. Mother was frantic, for we knew that the Nazi doctors loved to put people like me—who were no longer of much use to the Reich—in death camps. But I felt that I would slowly die anyway if I didn't get some medical help and a rest from the factory labor. Feeling trapped by the circumstances, we prayed for wisdom for several days. Noticing my condition, my supervisor scolded me daily for my dullness. I was petrified that I would be turned in for my poor performance in the factory and be severely reprimanded and punished. Although Mother and I prayed earnestly, by a week later my physical condition had only worsened. I began to turn a peaked yellow, and for three nights, I hardly slept. During one of those nights, I was haunted by a recurring dream that God seemed to impress on me. In the dream, I saw a gray, gloomy day with an overcast sky. Mother and I were in the dream, and she seemed to be packing a suitcase. In the next scene we stood on the shores of a giant body of water, and in the fog-shrouded distance I could see a giant ship crowded with people. They were waving good-bye. When I turned to question Mother about it, she was gone. I looked out to the ship again, and now Mother was on board! I called out to her, but it was too late because the ship had already weighed anchor. As it turned and sailed out to sea, Mother waved good-bye to me.

All the faces on that desperate ship were Jewish, and I knew clearly that they were headed for one of Hitler's camps. I also knew that someday the ship would come back for me. And though I longed for Mother to come back and stand with me on the seashore, I felt certain she would be safe when she reached her destination. At the same time I had a strange assurance that I, too, would be safe even if the ship capsized and sank. It was a peace that passed all understanding.

That week we heard that the Christian Jews of Breslau were still somewhat protected, so Mother insisted that I visit the company doctor. My stomach pain, nausea, and peaked color alarmed even my Nazi doctor, though he made sure he showed no sympathy.

"So you can't handle the work here; is that it?" he barked at me as he gazed through his thick glasses. I sat slumped in a chair in his office, trying to squelch the pain in the pit of my stomach.

"It's not the work, sir. I can handle it fine when I'm well."

"I'm told you are a good worker," he said. "We need hard workers like you to help us rebuild the Reich and add to its glorious future."

I couldn't understand why he would say such a strange thing to me. What possible part did I play in Germany's future? Laborers were probably a dime a dozen; and since my education had been thwarted, I could probably rise no further.

"By the looks of you," he continued, "you have yellow jaundice. I am going to send you home for a few weeks, but when you return, I'd better hear that you're working twice as hard. Go home now. I will call your supervisor."

God must have intervened, for the doctor could have written

me a prescription for a gas chamber.

"Heil Hitler!" he shouted at me as I made my way out of the examining room. I muffled a few nondescript words, but I would never utter the horrible "Heil Hitler."

* * *

The prospect of God's ultimate plan for my life was in my thoughts frequently while I fought for my health during the next few weeks at home. I knew that, in God's eyes, to die was gain, but I was sure I could serve Him more effectively by living. I wanted to be a *living* testimony to His grace and mercy in my life and to be able to encourage someone else by my life, not my death.

New hope surged within me—a hope that was almost as unexplainable as the peace I often felt. However, some of it was based on the German defeat in Africa and on the Russian front. Hope grew as Italy began to look as if she would falter and fall into the hands of the Allies.

Hope was present even in the midst of terrifying news: The Nazi ovens would be stoked and would receive more and more Jews in a final attempt to solve "the Jewish problem."

"Kill off the Jews like rats!" came the command. "Let the world take its cue from Germany!"

Our freedom would be short-lived.

I rested at home for four glorious weeks in an attempt to lick the jaundice. God surely knew that I needed to gain that strength for the ordeal that lay ahead. The summer of 1943 was the calm before my own personal storm.

I had turned sixteen that spring, and now mother seemed to be trying to push a wedge between us. I felt no lack of love from her; rather, she was attempting to teach me to stand on my own if need be. As Jewish Christians in Breslau, we lived in the eye of a hurricane, waiting for the inevitable storm. We basked in boredom and hard labor while still enjoying our relatively free status.

The only question that remained was whether Germany would be totally destroyed in the war. Every day she lost more ground and our execution was stayed a little longer. How we prayed that the Allies in all their victories could liberate some of the death camps. My heart ached for sweet fellowship with other believers, yet neither time nor circumstances allowed Mother and me the opportunity to have fellowship with other Christians. God Himself truly had to be our Friend and Companion, Counselor and Comforter.

As I rested at home, the soft breezes of summer blew into our tiny apartment. Mother and I had forgotten the unpleasantness of the winter elements and were simply enjoying the new and fresh life around us. We tried to enjoy the few pleasures we had left—our free evenings, our modest food rations, our togetherness. But as I rested, I strained to hear the sound of airplanes as they flew over Breslau. The memory of Berlin would always be with me. Just hearing the roar of a truck brought back visions of bombers streaming overhead in a darkened and panicked Berlin. Few cities of significance in Germany escaped the air attacks.

Pastor Hornig visited me several times during my stay at home, and suddenly one day the happy anticipation of his coming erased a host of my fears as well as my sadness. He, too, had grown old in the ten years of Nazi rule, but he hadn't lost his special love for Mother and me and the whole cause for which he was fighting and risking his life. Instead, his faith had grown stronger and his determination to aid Breslau's remaining Jews had increased.

Even though he could see the lingering effects of my jaundice and malnutrition, as he stood and looked at me for several seconds, the pastor exclaimed, "Anita, you have become a young woman in the last year! The child in you is gone."

I wasn't so sure I had ever had a childhood, for it had been obscured in all the confusion of the last ten years, but I knew how much I loved this wonderful man of God.

I threw my arms around Pastor Hornig, the only man who had been able to help me understand my heavenly Father's love for me.

The pastor risked his life every time he associated with the Jewish cause. He even risked it by walking into our ghetto and identifying himself so strongly with us.

"How can I turn against the people who wrote my precious Bible and who gave me my Savior?" he said to me as we visited. "The Jews are the apple of God's eye. Because Germany has harmed them, she will never be the same. She will never prosper again."

"Do you think it will all be over soon?" I asked, as if Pastor Hornig could predict such a turn of events.

"It is over now, Anita, but not officially. Germany is finished, but Hitler won't give up. He will hold out until the Russians stand on the steps of the parliament building and raise the Red flag. Realistically, that could be a year or two away. But it is certain that Hitler is too mad to surrender!"

"You should exercise more caution," I scolded. "You shouldn't be so blatant in your resistance."

Pastor Hornig smiled and sat back in our rickety rocking chair. "Mrs. Hornig and I are protected. God has His hand on us. We aid the Jews and refuse to place the Führer's picture on our church altar even though I am followed and the Gestapo sit through all of my services. But I must be honest with you, Anita. It is false security for you to think that you and your mother are safe because you are believers in Jesus; you are in danger. But never forget that Jesus is able to give you unexplainable peace no matter what the circumstances. The apostle Paul wrote about that. In spite of his beatings, jailings, and shipwrecks, he always had joy and peace. He told us to rejoice in the Lord always. Promise me you'll remember that."

"I will."

His visit was just what I needed, better than the most potent medicine. Perhaps it was even better than freedom, for freedom without the love of a godly man like Pastor Hornig wouldn't really be freedom. A true representative of Jesus, he breathed life and health back into me just by his presence, which told me his love for mother and me was very special. With this life-giving injection, I felt fortified to face the factory again in a week.

Mother informed me that I was to be transferred to the office of the wine-bottling factory, where I would be able to sit down and regain some strength. Someone at the factory had an ounce of compassion left and knew that more forced labor would just cause a recurrence of the jaundice.

I was grateful for my sit-down office work at the wine-bottling company, but I grieved for Mother, who hauled and lifted things all day long. Her body screamed with pain by the end of the day from the heavy, forced labor. I nearly requested a transfer back to the factory work so we could work side by side, but I feared a recurrence of the jaundice. Something buried deep within told me I might need all my strength later. Each week at the factory, some Jewish employees disappeared without explanation. Their fate was always left to our fanciful imagination.

Paradoxically, as Germany grew worse year after year, our Christmases grew better! We always had less, but whatever we did have, we appreciated ten times more. In 1943 we had Christmas Day off, and Mother and I attended services at the church. It was a glorious day as we breathed the fresh air and rode the streetcar through the light-falling snow. The war was so close to us and yet so far away. Italy had surrendered to the Allies and then declared war on Germany, too. The Red Army was pressing toward the Polish frontier.

The Nuremberg Laws were issued that winter, which added to our jubilant Christmas. These laws stated that a Jewish man or woman who had been married at one time to a German spouse was protected from the arrests and concentration camps, as long as he or she no longer believed in Judaism. Children born to such a marriage were also protected. But would Hitler break these laws as he had broken all the others? Only time would tell; Pastor Hornig cautioned us again not to be too optimistic. He already knew of some violations of the laws.

Dreams come and go, but the dream I had dreamt during the summer came to mind too frequently. *Could God be speaking to me through it?* I wondered. Was the ship real, or did it symbolize something? Could its recurring memory be a way of conditioning me for the time when its significance would be realized?

We tried to be thankful for each day. To look back brought only painful memories; to look forward brought fear and uncertainty, even though Mother and I knew that Jesus was with us. But we could cling to today and savor it—savor the clean air over Breslau and the fresh-fallen snow that as yet didn't have cinders of explosions and fire in it, as did the snow in Berlin and Hamburg and Cologne.

"God is greater than all the combined evil of the Third Reich," Pastor Hornig reminded us privately that Christmas Day. "He is in control of the war and in control of your lives, too. I feel He will preserve you and your mother, Anita, but you must be strong witnesses for Him everywhere."

I would hear Pastor Hornig's words a thousand times over in the course of my life.

We believers of St. Barbara's made a glorious, joyful noise unto the Lord that Christmas as we sang the Christmas carols that spoke of love, joy, and peace. Peace! Oh, that God would allow us to bask in it again soon.

Ye are of God, little children, and have overcome them: because greater is he that is in you, than he that is in the world.
—1 John 4:4

8

ǥood-bye, motḣer

It was 6:00 a.m. as Mother and I scurried around the apartment, getting ready to leave for the factory. It was an unusually gray late-January morning, and we dreaded the freezing streetcar ride and walk ahead of us. As I looked out the window into the predawn sky, I shuddered at the familiar sight. It was the same lead-gray, overcast sky that I had seen in my dream several months earlier! Only the shoreline and the ship in the distance were missing.

"Mother!" I called. "Something will happen today, I just know it. It is as if God has conveyed an unexplainable message to me."

"Don't be silly, Anita."

"I can't explain it," I said as I studied the sky for several minutes. "Do you remember the awful dream I told you about, Mother? I see the same sky this morning that I saw in my dream."

I paced and stalled as we prepared to leave. When the dawn struggled to break through, I ran to the window again. This time I saw the Gestapo police wagon drive up in front of our building!

"They're here, Mother!" I exclaimed. "This time it is for us! I know it because of my dream."

"We're protected by the Nuremberg Laws, Anita," Mother said too confidently. "Get your coat on now or we'll miss the streetcar."

I stood frozen in place as two men got out of the police wagon and marched up our front stairs. Could there be a remote chance that they were coming for one of the other few families in our building? Did I have the right to wish that awful fate on them just to save us?

The familiar marching steps came down our hall, but they didn't walk past our door. This time the command of "Open up!" was clearly for Mother and me, and finally Mother realized that my ominous feeling and dream had not been products of my runaway imagination.

"You were right, Anita," Mother said. She opened our door, and the two Gestapo agents pushed their way in. My heart raced with fear! *Jesus, where is that peace You promised?* I prayed silently. *Why is it that Mother and I are riveted with fear now?*

"We've come to arrest Hilde Dittman," the spokesman of the two barked as he looked at Mother. "You have three minutes to pack one bag. We will label your furniture, for it now belongs to the state."

"No!" I protested in futility. "We are Jewish Christians! We are protected by the law!"

"The Führer is the law, and we are obeying his wish. You thank him that he still is compassionate enough to let you have your freedom, kid. He only wants your mother this time."

"I'll be all right," Mother said, trying to reassure me.

The other Gestapo guard, who hadn't spoken, looked at me almost compassionately with his Aryan blue eyes. Maybe he'd had enough of war and hate, or maybe God had even touched his heart recently. His eyes weren't seductive or flirting; rather, they were soft and kind as he saw my panic and fear. Somehow he seemed to want to communicate his kindness as he stood with his arms folded, the snow from his boots melting on the floor.

"You'll have to sign these forms," the other man commanded Mother. "They release all your possessions to the state." He took some papers out of an envelope and placed them on the table for Mother.

"Where are you taking her?" I demanded.

"Down to the synagogue today. Tomorrow the whole lot of them will probably be sent to Theresienstadt in Czechoslovakia. You will be notified."

Reluctantly Mother signed their papers, releasing all our possessions to Germany. I was allowed to keep just a handful of items, including my bed. I would be allowed to buy back some of the other things from the state at greatly inflated prices.

"May I please speak to my daughter alone for a moment?" Mother asked.

"We have no time for that. She may come with us while we take you to the synagogue if she likes."

"May I have just a moment to use the bathroom, then?" Mother said.

"Hurry up!"

Mother looked at me and motioned with her eyes toward the bathroom. Then she silently walked to the bathroom and came out almost immediately. Again her body language told me that she had left something for me there.

"I'm coming with her," I said as Mother finished packing a few items in her bag.

While putting on my coat, I quickly ran into the bathroom and saw that Mother had left a small purse. Opening it, I found the equivalent of nearly one hundred dollars in cash—no doubt her life savings that she had earmarked for a day such as today.

Finally the flood of tears came as I stood in the bathroom. Falling to my knees on the floor, I poured out my heart to Jesus. I desperately needed that inexplicable peace that I'd experienced before. It was one thing to mouth hopeful thoughts as the world around me went mad; it was something else to say it when that madness entered my own home.

"Hurry up!" came that familiar and impatient voice. Hearing the door open, I got up off my knees to join Mother as she was taken to the synagogue.

"What did Pastor Hornig say, Anita?" she reminded me. "He said God would protect us as long as we proclaimed His Word. Do you believe it, Anita?"

I wiped my tears on my coat sleeve as we turned out the lights. Mother picked up her small brown bag, and with her other hand she grasped my hand. The Gestapo men walked behind us as we left the apartment for the synagogue. I reflected on the many times Mother and I had huddled in our apartment while a family or an individual in our building was being taken away. Now it was our turn to experience the tragedy.

I envisioned the few remaining Jews in our neighborhood peering out their windows to see the sad sight. For those who didn't know the awesome power of God's protection, it must have been muted panic.

I held Mother's hand as the wagon sped off down the street, heading for the same synagogue where I had once visited Joachim. Mother and I couldn't speak as we went through Breslau. Instead, we kept our thoughts to ourselves and prayed that God would bring this bad dream to a swift end. Mother's grip on my hand told me not to be afraid. But I was only sixteen, and now I would be utterly alone in Hitler's hell. Even with the Hornigs and the believers at the church, it wouldn't be the same as having a close family member.

Mother was so unbelievably brave and calm that I wondered if God was ministering to her heart and giving her quiet assurance that His hand was over her. I pushed out the nagging voice of Satan that tried to tell me God had finally given up on the Jews and had left them to work out their own destiny.

As the familiar synagogue came into view, I remembered when I had told Joachim good-bye under similar circumstances. I had thought about and prayed for him nearly every day, wondering what further tragedy it would take before he believed in Jesus. I had trusted Joachim to Jesus, so why couldn't I trust Mother to Him now?

The police wagon came to a slow stop in front of the synagogue gate, and the Gestapo officers came around to help us out. I looked into the eyes of the guard who had earlier looked at me compassionately.

"May I go inside with her?" I asked him.

He hesitated and glanced at the other Gestapo policeman, who had already climbed back into the wagon.

"For only a moment," he said softly. "Hurry."

Mother and I walked several yards to the front door of the synagogue-turned-prison. For some reason I couldn't release her and send her across the threshold of the building, affirming her total loss of freedom. Besides, a sixteen-year-old should not have to give up her mother on the whim of a lunatic dictator!

We embraced for several long seconds on the steps of the synagogue. I knew that inside the building huddled a mass of despairing people—most of them without hope. At least Mother and I had that!

"Don't despair, Anita," Mother comforted. "The war will be over before the Nazis do away with me. You obey their every order; do you hear? You work hard at the factory and do whatever they want, short of denying God. I gave you your father's phone number if you want to call him. He might be able to help you. Maybe he can send you some money to buy back your things. The Gestapo guard is coming to get you now," she said as she looked over my shoulder. "Do as he says. Remember how much I love you."

Mother kissed me on the cheek and went inside the synagogue as the Gestapo man with the soft blue eyes came and took me by the arm.

"You must go now," he said. "You will be notified where your mother is being sent."

With that he escorted me to the gate and gently pushed me outside. His eyes looked sadly into mine as he closed the gate and locked it.

"I'm sorry," I heard him say ever so faintly.

Wasn't he used to this scene yet? He surely wasn't the hardened Aryan that Hitler wanted him to be.

I stared for several long minutes as the door to Mother's freedom closed.

As I trudged aimlessly through the slush and snow, I wallowed in my own grief and self-pity. I fought to remember the comforting words Pastor Hornig had told me in the past. He had me memorize the Twenty-third Psalm at one time, and now I tried to bring it to mind. I decided to head for Pastor Hornig's, where I would call to notify my supervisor at work and be comforted by the pastor's wise words.

Later that morning I sat with Pastor Hornig in the front row of the church sanctuary. We sat silently for a few moments as he groped for the right words to say.

"The believers here at the church will be your temporary family, Anita," he finally said. "I know it is not the same, but we will try to love you as much as Hilde does, and we will pray every day that she will come home soon. Remember, you're really not alone. Even without me or the church you wouldn't be alone, for God will never leave you."

I didn't take my eyes off the cross hanging at the front of the church.

"It's that cross, Anita," Pastor Hornig continued, "that enables you and me to endure anything, because Jesus conquered all manner of evil and wickedness on that cross. He is the Victor in the end. Because of His shed blood, all of Satan's efforts can be defeated if we but claim the power of the cross in our lives. The shed blood of Jesus is the strongest weapon we have in the world. You must appropriate it now."

Inside St. Barbara's Lutheran Church

"She was very brave," I said.

"Of course she was. Your mother knows that even if she walks through the valley of the shadow of death, she need not fear any evil. She told me once that if they ever came for her, her only real fear would be for you. That is why you must correspond with her every week and assure her that you're all right and doing well. Where are they taking her?"

"Theresienstadt, maybe."

"She can receive mail and packages there. You send her some food every week, Anita. She will need it because she will work long hours there and probably get little food. Often the guards let family members visit the prisoners the night before they go off to camp. Why don't you take your mother some food tonight at the synagogue? It is worth a try. Go next door and have Mrs. Hornig wrap up some sandwiches for you and your mother. I will call your supervisor and explain things to him. You may spend the day with us if you wish."

Hope welled up inside me once more as I entertained the thought of seeing mother again that evening. Mrs. Hornig prepared some sandwiches and fruit for us. I also wanted to take Mother her bathrobe that she'd forgotten, so I left the Hornigs to go home and put everything together and spend a few hours alone with my thoughts.

I could sense the prayers of the believers as Pastor Hornig spread the word about my situation. I was sure that eventually a sense of calm would replace the ache in my heart, for I knew that the believers from the church would be praying especially on behalf of Mother, me, and some other Jewish believers who were picked up that day.

Our dingy apartment seemed even more sterile as I walked into it toward noon. Mother's obvious absence screamed at me from every corner of the room. I knew she would want the warm bathrobe she'd forgotten in her haste, so I carefully packed a bag with the robe, the sandwiches, and fruit. I planned to take the streetcar back to the synagogue in the late afternoon, with the hope that I could see Mother one last time before she left for Theresienstadt early the next morning.

I paced the floor and then sat in the rocker. Intermittently I prayed and read the precious Bible that Pastor Hornig had given me years earlier. After impatiently watching the January sun begin to set, I finally left for the synagogue about four o'clock that afternoon. The streetcar would probably soon be crowded with people coming home from work, but I simply couldn't wait any longer. Maybe my mission was an exercise in futility; perhaps the guards would turn me away and thwart my wish to see Mother once more.

The setting sun peeked over the horizon just enough to reveal about a dozen other teenagers crowding around the entrance gate to the synagogue. I walked more quickly and my heart virtually skipped a few beats when I saw some familiar faces. Steffi Bott along with Gerhard, Wolfgang, and Rudi Wolf were there— their mothers were good friends of Mother's. I soon learned that they had been picked up too. Mrs. Bott and Mrs. Wolf were also Jewish believers. Circumstances in Germany hadn't allowed their children to become my close friends, but the present situation would draw us to each other. All of them also had been left by their Aryan fathers, and their Jewish mothers had become Christians recently. Apparently many of Breslau's Jewish believers had been picked up today.

"Steffi!" I exclaimed as I drew closer.

"Anita!"

"Can we go in?" I asked excitedly.

"No," she answered, "the guards won't let any of us in."

We nervously observed the situation from outside the gate. By now about twenty-five teenagers were pacing around the entrance gate, wanting to see their mothers one last time. Many of them held a bag or a small suitcase, probably containing food or clothing that their mothers would need. Some cried and some cursed; few accepted the situation very well. But it almost instantly drew Steffi, the Wolf brothers, and me together, since our mothers were all friends.

We all peered through the bars of the entrance gate to see if we could spot any of our mothers through the synagogue windows. Then Rudi Wolf looked curiously at the building adjoining the synagogue, currently a hotel, and I could tell his mind was working.

"There must be a connecting tunnel," Rudi finally said to us. "Let's go in the hotel and try to find it."

We were young, daring, and desperate. The fact that our suspicious behavior could be grounds for our own arrest made little difference to any of us.

"I'll go up to the clerk and ask for a phony name," Rudi said. "You try to find the stairs that lead to the basement while he's looking for the name. Once we find the basement, there must be a tunnel that leads to the synagogue."

We didn't even question the plan. Instead, the five of us

marched up the hotel stairs. Apparently the hotel had at one time been a school associated with the synagogue; but since all the Jewish schools had been closed recently, it had been turned into a hotel.

Steffi, Gerhard, and I hung back while Rudi and Wolfgang walked up to the hotel clerk and asked for the fictitious name. When the clerk turned to study his book, the three of us scanned the lobby for some stairs that would lead downstairs. Spotting a door that looked like it might lead to the basement, we quietly made our way there. As the clerk continued to look for the name, we sneaked slyly through the door. Sure enough, inside the door were the stairs that led to the hotel basement. We wound around the endless flight of stairs, dodging the dead cockroaches that littered the stairs. We ran down them so fast that we were nearly out of breath when we finally hit the bottom. At the foot of the stairs was the tunnel door! I felt God must be in the scheme to direct us so quickly.

"This is it!" Gerhard exclaimed. "This will take us to the synagogue."

"Are you sure we should do this?" Steffi finally said cautiously. "Maybe we should try the guards once more."

Gerhard didn't answer but forged ahead into the pitch-black tunnel. It was so black that it almost looked like a dark wall in front of us; but as we felt our way along, we knew it was the corridor that adjoined the other building.

I didn't care that I could be trapping myself permanently in the synagogue. I didn't care that I could get a police record for this act of rebellion. All I cared about was a chance to see Mother one more time and give her the food, the bathrobe, and my love.

We moved along silently now, feeling our way in the darkness. If we never returned, at least Rudi and Wolfgang would know what had happened and would report us to our few remaining friends or family. I prayed silently as we inched along the tunnel. We moved without speaking, Gerhard leading us carefully so we would not walk into something in the darkness.

Our steps sounded hollow in the tunnel, and even our heavy breathing seemed to resound off the walls. The tunnel couldn't be but a few yards long, yet it seemed as if an eternity had gone by since we began the uncertain venture.

At last, we heard faint voices in the distance and saw a crack of light. The voices grew louder and the light brighter as we neared the basement of the synagogue. Finally, we came to a door that was open just a crack, and we saw some of the prisoners milling about the synagogue basement. As Gerhard peered through the open crack in the door, he saw a Gestapo guard planted right in the middle of the prisoners.

"What shall we do?" Steffi whispered. Gerhard mouthed the word *wait*.

We were prepared to wait all night if we had to so that we might say good-bye to our mothers once more. Peeking through the door, we didn't recognize any of the women. Suddenly the guard started moving around and passed just inches from us. Gerhard could have reached out and touched his ugly brown uniform. We stood silently and held our breath for at least half an hour as the guard walked about restlessly. Finally he climbed some stairs leading to the main floor of the synagogue.

Gerhard opened our door a little wider and called to one of the women prisoners.

"Over here!" he whispered loudly.

The startled lady looked at us, amazed that we had come out of nowhere.

"We want to see our mothers once more," Gerhard continued. "They're Mrs. Wolf, Mrs. Dittman, and Mrs. Bott. Do you know where they are? Could you send them down here to the basement so we can give them some things?

"You will be arrested," the confused woman said. "Don't be

foolish; the guard will be back momentarily. He hasn't left us since early this morning."

"You must hurry, then!" Gerhard pleaded. "We want to give them these packages."

Gerhard took the three packages and set them on the floor of the synagogue basement.

"Here they are. If we get caught, will you promise you'll deliver the packages to Mrs. Bott, Mrs. Dittman, and Mrs. Wolf?"

The old woman nodded her head.

"What are you doing here?" came an angry voice from the other end of the tunnel. Then a flashlight appeared and we heard the steps of Nazi boots coming down the tunnel behind us.

"We've been found!" Steffi cried.

Chills ran down all of us. A glaring flashlight shone in our eyes now, and finally the form of a Nazi Gestapo officer appeared from the other end of the tunnel.

"You will all be arrested for this act of treason!" he yelled as the flashlight glared in my face.

"We only wanted to see our mothers once more," I pleaded. "We wanted to deliver some food to them, sir; that's all."

"Come with me," he said. "I caught your friends upstairs. I'm turning you all over to the Gestapo head."

We marched back through the tunnel, guided by the flashlight this time. No one spoke a word. We silently hoped the lady prisoner would deliver the packages to our mothers and tell them of our desperate attempt to see them once more. The disposition of the Gestapo head would determine our penalty.

When we reached the hotel lobby, we were joined by Rudi and Wolfgang and then escorted by two men to the Gestapo office. Next we were taken by truck to the office of a Mr. Hampel, a short, squatty man with vicious eyes who scowled at our daring persistence to see our mothers.

After lining us up against a wall in his office, Mr. Hampel paced back and forth in front of us for a full five minutes. The anger inside him churned. Out of the corner of my eye, I could see Steffi trembling, and I knew she was ready to break into tears. Gerhard, Wolfgang, and Rudi wanted to protect us, but they were helpless.

The tension grew as Mr. Hampel paced and shot angry looks our way. "You five are guilty of a major crime," he said. "You tried to free prisoners, and that is punishable by death."

"No," Rudi pleaded, "we only wanted to say good-bye to our mothers. We each had a bag of food for them that we left with an old lady in the synagogue basement."

The unspoken fear, of course, was that our mothers could be punished for our attempt—which had not occurred to us in the beginning.

"I love my mother!" Steffi exclaimed as she broke into tears. "I just wanted to see her once more. We had no escape plan."

"That's all any of us wanted," Gerhard insisted. "Our mothers would never have gone along with what we did. It was all our idea."

"I have no time for your silly sentimentality," Mr. Hampel replied. "I am going to discuss this with someone. You will all remain here."

Mr. Hampel sent in another guard to watch us and keep us from talking. The guard sat in Mr. Hampel's chair and didn't take his glaring eyes off us as we stood erect along the wall. I was sure we were all praying silently through the tears and our fear.

About thirty minutes later Mr. Hampel returned. Storming noisily into his office, he blurted out, "You are all on the Gestapo's blacklist. If any of you does the slightest wrong thing, it will cost you your lives. You will be watched every day. Get out of here now!"

"Thank you, sir," Rudi exclaimed. "God's blessing on you, Mr. Hampel."

We silently filed out into the cold, dark night. After walking quickly for a block, we all stopped and broke into tears of relief and thankfulness as we embraced one another.

"We shall always be friends," I said as we shared our joy. "We must always do everything we can for each other and meet often to encourage one another and pray for our mothers. We have so much to be thankful for today."

The unspoken reality was that the Nuremberg law protecting Jews once married to Germans was phony, and our time would be up eventually, too. Our earnest prayer was for a swift end to the war. If a prison camp awaited us, we prayed it would be with our mothers.

Now, along with the believers of my church, I had a new family: the Wolf brothers and Steffi Bott. Tragedy had united us in such a way that we couldn't be separated.

When thou passest through the waters, I will be with thee; and through the rivers, they shall not overflow thee: when thou walkest through the fire, thou shalt not be burned; neither shall the flame kindle upon thee.
—Isaiah 43:2

9

ZWIEBACK BREAD

mother's going left a crater of emptiness in my heart. I couldn't concentrate at work, and I was so lonely I couldn't eat; besides, I saved most of my rations for Mother. It was confirmed she had been sent to Camp Theresienstadt in Czechoslovakia, where she could get food packages once a week.

One morning before I left for work, the Gestapo knocked on my door again. This time, however, they came to collect all of Mother's possessions that the state had claimed. They took everything but my bed and a half dozen small items. Because the Gestapo insisted that most of my possessions belonged to Mother, they allowed me the "privilege" of buying some of my things back at greatly inflated prices.

I didn't put up any fuss while two men pushed their way inside and started putting my things in boxes. They looked at me curiously for some time before one of them finally spoke up.

"How old are you, kid?" he asked, not interrupting his working pace.

"I'll be seventeen in May," I answered.

"Other kids your age would be upset if we came into their home and did this. Why not you?"

"Hysteria won't bring Mother back or allow me to keep my

things," I replied calmly. "My strength comes from God. He's in control of Germany and of my life."

He rolled his eyes at the other Gestapo officer and kept packing. Then, in several trips, they hauled out the furniture and boxes, leaving the apartment stripped and bare. They took tables, lamps, and even rugs, until I had only a shell of a room.

As I was putting my coat on to leave for work, they finally carried out the last confiscated item. "You can keep what's left," one of them said to me. "Some of what we've taken you can buy back." He handed me a piece of paper on which was written the inflated price of my things.

"Come to the local Gestapo office and pay this amount. If you don't come within five days, the state will keep the things or sell them to someone else."

Neither the church nor my puny salary could possibly pay that terribly overpriced figure for my furniture and other possessions.

As I rode the streetcar to the factory that morning, I searched for an answer. Then I remembered that Mother had given me Father's phone number for just such a situation. We hadn't seen one another in years. Maybe the war had softened him and he would be responsive to my dilemma. I felt it was a risk just to call him, simply because I didn't think I could stand one more ounce of rejection. But fortified and confident of being loved by Mother, Steffi, Gerhard, Wolfgang, Rudi, and the church members, I decided to take that risk and seek Father's help.

That night after work I went to Pastor Hornig's home to make the long-distance telephone call to Father, who had remarried and moved to Sorau, about sixty-five miles away. I frankly told the pastor about my bitterness and resentment toward Father.

"Anita," Pastor Hornig said, "it could be that your forgiving love will win him to Jesus. You cannot blame a man for buckling under the pressure of the Nazis. It was his life or yours."

I dialed the number Mother had scratched on the piece of paper. Then I waited anxiously for Father's familiar voice, feeling terribly awkward.

"It's Anita," I said as he answered the phone.

It seemed like an eternity before he responded, sounding pleasantly surprised at hearing my voice.

"Mother's been taken to Theresienstadt in Czechoslovakia," I continued.

"I'm so sorry," Father said. "Is there anything I can do?"

Encouraged by his compassion, I surged ahead.

"Yes. You could help me buy back my possessions that the Nazis confiscated today. They inflated their worth to over a thousand marks,* and I have only five days to pay it or they will give them to someone else."

"Anita, you must believe me when I say I regret everything that has happened. Of course I'll help you. Have you heard any news of Hella?"

"No, there is no mail from England."

"I will send you the money in the morning. Anita, will you keep in touch with me? Perhaps you could spend some time with us here in Sorau. The war hasn't hit here, and it's quiet. It might be safer here."

Father's genuine concern impressed me. I told him about the money Mother had left me and that I had heard a prisoner's freedom could be bought. I hoped to do this for Mother if I got the chance. After all, it was her money. He accepted that.

"I'm doing office work in a factory," I said. "Perhaps I could come if I get some time off. Remember, I have only five days to buy back my things, so please hurry."

Mother's absence had put a longing in my heart for Father's love, and I knew God was at work trying to heal my huge wound of bitterness and resentment against him.

* About five dollars.

* * *

During the spring of 1944, Steffi, Gerhard, Rudi, Wolfgang, and I met often to share news of our mothers. We were allowed to write to them and send parcels of food, but every letter or package was censored.

Frequently after work I would go to the dairy store, the butcher shop, and the vegetable store. The owners knew me quite well, and they knew Mother had been sent to Theresienstadt. I explained to them that I sent Mother almost all the food I purchased with my ration cards. As a result, they often slipped in a little extra for me that exceeded the amount on my ration card. Sometimes it was just an extra egg or a hunk of cheese or an extra potato, but I was very thankful for anything. Since it took about ten days for a parcel to arrive, I sent Mother only nonperishable items.

The food I saved for myself was less than a starvation diet. In the morning, I had a roll and a cup of coffee. I didn't eat lunch, simply telling everyone at work I was dieting. In the evening I might have a bowl of soup or some lettuce. Often I baked bread or a cake, but I always sent it to Mother; her postcards told me of her inexpressible joy upon receiving the food.

I survived on starvation rations for months, but never lost one pound, became sick, or missed a day of work. God just nourished me supernaturally in a way I will never be able to understand.

That spring Germany suffered more massive blows in the war, and her cities continued to burn as the air war intensified. Breslau still escaped being bombed, but we had to comply with strict blackout regulations that required car lights to be dimmed, lamps to be shielded, and windows to be covered with thick shades and drapes.

Gradually other teenagers joined our little group to share news from their mothers in Theresienstadt. Many of them were unbelievers, and we tried to share our faith with them, pointing to the many miracles in our lives that had revealed God's sovereignty and protection of us. We took turns reading the postcards sent by our mothers, rejoicing or weeping together over the news. However, very little about the camp's harsh conditions was allowed to go through the mail. Most of the postcards were brief; our mothers simply sent their love and told us our packages had arrived.

As June approached, I knew I must send Mother something special for her birthday. I longed to send her roses, but she would understand the best I could do was to send wild hyacinths. I did, however, bake her a birthday cake filled with raisins. I also got her some plums and apples, then wrapped everything in a nice package. I prayed a special prayer over the package as I wrapped it, asking that it would arrive exactly on her birthday. Two weeks later a postcard told me it had arrived on that very day.

The Allies landed in Normandy that month. Rumor had it that everyone who had even one Jewish grandparent was now going to be picked up in a last-ditch effort to wipe out the Jewish race. Hitler would make the Jews pay, of course, for his mistakes in the war, a pattern that was never broken.

In late June, I awoke early one sultry morning with an overwhelming compulsion to rush to the bakery and buy some zwieback toast. *How absurd!* I thought. Yet something told me Mother desperately needed zwieback that week and not the usual pumpernickel I'd always sent. Pumpernickel was her favorite, and it seldom turned moldy in the slow mail delivery.

Yet I couldn't deny the inner impulse to rush to the bakery after work that evening and send mother the zwieback. As I sent it off, I prayed a special prayer for extra speed.

Sometime later I got a postcard from Mother that explained my premonition. She had been ill and was nearly dying from dysentery, and she'd yearned for some zwieback bread to help her condition. In the crude concentration camp's barracks, she got down on her knees and prayed that God would impress her need on my heart.

The toast arrived with record-breaking speed, and because of it, her health was restored.

Mother had been in Theresienstadt nearly seven months, and I had become quietly resigned to fighting for life on my own, knowing my heavenly Father watched over me and loved me more than any earthly parent. I saw how He gave me the wisdom of an adult, though I was only seventeen. I had incredible peace that what I had prayed would be a reality. It remained even after I heard the horror stories about the Nazi concentration camps. Escaped prisoners brought back the truth about the death camps and prisons, while others smuggled out coded messages to loved ones. By and large, the German people didn't know of the pain and slaughter in the camps, for the Nazis tried to keep the facts about them from the world.

But the stories from the camps told of massive gassings and shootings. Following a gassing, the bodies would be cremated in giant ovens. Giant smokestacks coughed out soot from burning bodies, blanketing most of Europe. Fellow prisoners, or in some cases family members, would then be ordered to break up the remaining bones and bury them in mass graves.

In some camps, the prisoners were worked to death. In others they were left to starve to death; or sometimes life-giving medical care and drugs were withheld from them.

Word leaked out of the massive killing of some three million Russian prisoners of war. Frequently the Russian prisoners were put in hastily built "cages," because there wasn't room for all of them in the camps. The healthy, the sick, and the dying were forced together. Later, to stop the spread of disease, flamethrowers were turned on the cages, destroying both the dead bodies and the living prisoners.

We also knew that much of the soap being used by Germans had been made from the human fat of prisoners, and human hair stuffed many a mattress. Germany's gold reserves were increased with the gold fillings taken from dead prisoners' teeth.

The worst horrors took place in Auschwitz, from which few ever escaped or lived to tell their stories. It was estimated that almost three million already had perished there, and at the end of the war it would be learned that 80 percent of those sent to Auschwitz died.

View of part of the fortification called the Ravelin and the Gestapo prison courtyard in the Small Fortress at Theresienstadt. *Courtesy United States Holocaust Memorial Museum*

The most gruesome story leaked out early in 1944 and would later be documented. Hitler informed Himmler that it was not enough for the Jews to die; they must die in agony, for they were only germs, not people. Himmler was ordered to devise a plan to make thousands of Jews die a horrible death. He got the idea of placing Jewish prisoners in freight cars having their floors coated with a layer of dehydrated calcium oxide. The substance caused terrible burns, and prisoners often suffered for days before dying an awful death in the freight cars, which were left in a secluded place.

Hitler had only to whisper and ten thousand prisoners would die that day.

But the thing that would shock the German people soon was that many of their own people—their sick, elderly, and insane were

Auschwitz. *Courtesy United States Holocaust Memorial Museum*

also being cruelly exterminated.

But good news as well came in mid-1944. An attempt had been made to assassinate the Führer. The Allies began to score significant victories, including their entrance into Paris, Brussels, and Holland. The Soviets continued to make great gains, while Rumania and Bulgaria struggled to break free and declare war on Germany. It all added up to hope, and the true Christians in Germany, and surely around the world, fell to their knees again to pray for a swift end to the war.

German cities by the dozens lay in total, smoldering ruins as the Red Army Federation and the Americans continued to score direct hits all over Germany's pockmarked landscape. For every act of ruthless German air aggression against the Allies, they retaliated with even more destructive force. Uncounted hundreds of thousands perished in German cities. At first the survivors dug out bravely and quietly and began to rebuild their cities and factories, hardly questioning the Führer, who surely knew what was best for Germany. But gradually the fighting German spirit waned. In one raid, one hundred thousand Germans could be blown to pieces.

The human mind and body could not logically withstand such pressures and uncertainties, especially if a person had a loved one in a camp or if he himself was on the Nazi blacklist. Added to the other horrors was the constant threat that a death-camp experience awaited him after a harsh midnight knock on his door. The Nazi blacklist included more than just Jews. Christians who were suspected of hiding or aiding Jews were also on it, as well as anyone who uttered an anti-Nazi sentiment. A time would come for all of us to be hauled off to death camps unless the Allies—with God's help—could rescue us.

One day, as I did my routine filing at the factory, I was lost in thought. My stomach growled embarrassingly, for I had sent all of the previous two days' rations to Mother at Theresienstadt. She had gotten almost all of my food rations over the last months.

"There's a young lady who wants to speak to you, Miss Dittman," came my boss's cautious voice. He kept a suspicious eye on me as I went to the telephone. It was my good friend Steffi, whose voice sounded almost hysterical.

"I've been summoned to be at the railway station at 10:00 a.m. tomorrow, Anita!" came her breathy voice. "You will probably have a summons, too, when you get home tonight. Oh, Anita, I'm so frightened!"

Steffi and I had grown very close since our mothers had been hauled away to Theresienstadt seven months earlier. In a sense, we were a family to each other—closer than Hella and I had ever been. "It's all right, Steffi. We'll go together, then. God has protected us so far. Besides, the war should soon be—" I stopped speaking abruptly. How foolish of me to risk saying something like that!

"Cling tightly to Jesus' hand tonight, Steffi."

The Gestapo summons awaited me when I arrived home from work that evening. A summons rather than an abrupt knock on the door was perhaps in deference to our having one Aryan parent. The insanity of the war contained such absurdities. I was to report to the railroad station at 10:00 a.m. with just one small piece of baggage. Our time had finally arrived. It was inevitable, for people with far less Jewish blood had been taken months ago. Only God had kept the Nazis from sending me the summons earlier.

"Oh, dear Jesus," I whispered as I threw myself on my bed and buried my face in the pillow that evening, "I believe You can give me the strength to go through this ordeal. You are always testing my faith. Dear Jesus, show me how to tell Mother I'm being taken. She must know so she can pray for me and so she will know why the food parcels I've been sending will stop."

My pillow was wet with tears. I had no way to get word to Pastor Hornig before leaving in the morning. By the time he found out, I'd be well on my way to some unknown destination. Yet word would get to him quickly, and he would pray to God for my protection every day. I knew the effective prayers of the Christians in the church would be with me for the difficult journey that lay ahead.

I had to smuggle a note to Mother about my arrest. Perhaps I could bury a note in a loaf of bread. Yes, it was worth a try! If I hurried, the bakery would still be open. I raced to the bakery a few blocks away, darting in and out between weary people coming home from work. Their faces told me they knew Germany was losing the war. Even if no one verbalized it, they all had quietly resigned themselves to it.

I bought a two-pound loaf of pumpernickel bread and ran home to complete my main task before leaving in the morning. The loaf of bread had a thick company label on it, which was just perfect. I carefully peeled off the label and cut a small hole in the bread, just large enough to slip in a small note to Mother, which read:

Mother, I'm going off to a camp tomorrow, so I won't be sending you any food for a while. Don't worry about me. I will be all right. We'll soon be reunited! Love, Anita.

I carefully pressed the rolled-up note into the loaf of bread and then replaced the label to cover the hole. As I finished wrapping the loaf of bread, an amazing calm fell over my body. It was as if the hand of God had been placed on my shoulder, and His soothing voice was saying, *"Anita, trust only in Me, and I will never leave you nor forsake you. Though you walk through the valley of the shadow of death, you need not fear any evil, for I am with you."*

As instructed, I put a few belongings into my knapsack: a small pan, a bowl, a spoon and fork, soap, a towel, and one change of clothes. I neatly wrapped the Bible Pastor Hornig gave me and included it. I knew it might be taken away from me, but I would try to keep it. Then I lay down on my bed to think and to pray. It was a hot, sticky August night, one that would normally keep me awake for a breath of cool air or for the sound of an air-raid siren. Humanly speaking, it made absolutely no sense that I had the most peaceful sleep of my young life, in spite of the ordeal which I knew lay before me.

Shortly before ten o'clock the next morning I saw Steffi at the depot. As soon as we saw one another, we ran to each other and embraced. Steffi began to cry again, and I took her hand as we waited for instructions.

"All of this is happening with God's permission," I assured her. "He has given me absolute assurance that we will be all right—even that we will be reunited with our mothers soon! Don't despair so easily, Steffi. Where is your faith?"

"It was never like yours, Anita," she sniffled. "You must have it for both of us." She set her suitcase down and rubbed away the tears, which made her cheeks glow in the hot morning sun. I held tightly to her other hand. Everywhere frightened people pushed, hurried, and then waited. I recognized many of them, including the Wolf brothers, from all my years of living in Breslau. Most were like Steffi and me and had only one parent who was Jewish.

God was gracious to include other believers in this trainload of frightened human cargo. I recognized several whom Pastor Hornig had led to Jesus. Some of us had thus far escaped the camps because we weren't the typical Jew; instead, we believed in Jesus. We'd been seen participating in Protestant church services. In the Nazis' eyes, our blood was dirty and far from perfect Aryan, but they didn't consider us bacteria, as they did the Jews who had gone before us.

However, some of those at the train station were practicing Jews who had been called in a last-minute Nazi effort to rid Germany and the world of Jews once and for all.

Frightened, "impure" human beings were herded onto the train by screaming SS men who paraded up and down with rifles and pistols. The train's passenger seats and sooty windows were slick with black dirt from the ashes of burning Germany, but at least we weren't being shoved into a cattle car, as many of our relatives had been. As the SS men barked out commands, Steffi and I inched forward to board and find a place to sit. We talked freely but avoided any conversation or inflection that would be interpreted as anti-Nazi.

"Where do you think we are going?" Steffi questioned as we plopped down side by side on the train.

"Maybe to some work camp," I answered as I set my knapsack on my lap. "It won't be a long stay, Steffi."

Sniffles and moans could be heard throughout our car, the sounds seeming to cover the whole gamut of human despair. It was as though a satanic cloud had hung over the Reich for more than ten years, and now all its demons of fear and despair had been let loose to occupy any hearts that didn't know Jesus!

The Nazis were convinced that Jews around the world were blowing the war trumpet and that because of their birth and race, they all were members of an international conspiracy against Nazi Germany. Every living Jew was an enemy of Germany. If Jews were meek and passive and not aggressive, Hitler insisted it was out of cowardice, not because their hearts were free of hatred for Germany. The contempt of the whole nation of Germany was heaped upon anyone who aided or loved a Jew as well. I lived in fear for Pastor Hornig, for few German men did what he did for the Jews.

The Wolf brothers sat behind Steffi and me. Rudi leaned forward to whisper something to us. "I overheard the SS men," he said quietly. "We're going to Camp Barthold near Schmiegrode. It's a work camp." He leaned back in his seat as a uniformed SS man marched down the aisle, counting heads.

As the train inched out of Breslau, I peeked into my knapsack to see if my little Bible was still there. Should we be denied physical food, I wanted to be sure we had spiritual food. "We have a great big God, Steffi," I said softly. Steffi stared ahead, expressionless. She appeared to be on the brink of losing touch with reality, and I quickly prayed for her. In an instant her glazed eyes flashed again, and she looked at me. I pointed to the Bible that was wrapped in brown paper in my knapsack, and we both smiled.

We rolled along the German countryside for two hours. I was amazed to see so little destruction, even though I knew the Allies had been concentrating their assault on the major cities. Few of the big cities had escaped the terrible nightly air raids; Dresden was the lone city that stood intact. How long that would last, we had no idea. But the rolling, green hills and fields were almost tranquil. I wondered if the farmers knew that horrible suffering existed just miles away, that most of the cities were becoming smoldering skeletons, that victims lay in huge numbers under the rubble, and that many of the living wandered homeless. I wondered if the farmers knew as they peered out of their farmhouse windows at the passing train that the Nazis considered its cargo to be of less value than the cattle that grazed peacefully on the hillsides. I wondered if those very farmers went to church on Sunday and prayed to the Jewish (and Gentile) God, but at the same time spurned the Jews.

We rode silently, most of us too fearful to talk. I watched as the faces in my car stared blankly, frozen with uncertainty. How thankful I was for the inner peace that gripped me, giving me an indefinable assurance that God was in total control, not just of our lives, but of Germany, the Allied countries, and all the war-weary world.

When the train stopped at the village of Schmiegrode, we poured out, many being prodded along with gun butts. The men were sent off in one direction and the women in another. Three armed guards escorted about 150 of us women over cobblestone streets for several blocks, and then we entered a wooded area. We walked for some distance—a mile perhaps—to a weather-beaten work camp that was nothing more than a huge cow barn, a horse stable, and a main building for the Nazi staff. The cow barn would be the women's dormitory, and the horse stable the men's quarters. Remaining silent, we walked swiftly, entering the gate and then standing in formation as directed.

After a head count, the women were herded into the barn and ordered to stand at quiet attention while an SS guard gave us instructions. He scowled at us and marched up and down authoritatively in front of our formation. None of us could have known the horrors ahead.

For I am persuaded, that neither death, nor life, nor angels, nor principalities, nor powers, nor things present, nor things to come, nor height, nor depth, nor any other creature, shall be able to separate us from the love of God, which is in Christ Jesus our Lord.
—Romans 8:38–39

10

WORK CAMP

"This is your new home," said the SS guard, a twisted smile on his face. "I hope you like it. You have little choice." He sneered as he laughed at us.

"You will sleep on the straw on the floor," he continued. "Each of you will be issued two horse blankets. You can put one on the ground over the straw, and you may sleep anywhere in the barn. Outside is a cold-water faucet. You may bathe by putting water from the faucet into a bucket we will provide, or you may bathe in the creek if you like. The toilet is out back. It is just an open ditch, but it is good enough for you." He stopped talking but continued to march up and down.

"Starting tomorrow morning you will be put to work. The Führer looks very favorably on hard workers. Since the German working day has been extended to ten hours, yours will be too. It will be hard labor for some. We will awaken you at 4:00 a.m., and you will stand in formation out in the yard in the center of camp, where you will be counted and given a slice of bread. Then you will march a few kilometers to the work area. It is about an hour away by foot. Most of you will dig ditches that will stop the Russian tanks that head our way. Your evenings will be free for you to do as you wish. We will appoint one group leader for every ten women, and your leader will get a bucket for you to use to wash your dishes, your clothes, and yourselves. We have a small ration of soap we will give you, but it must last many weeks. We can give you no luxuries, and you must give us an honest day's labor. For your labor, we will pay you twenty marks a month. I hope you appreciate our generosity, for nowhere else in Germany do prisoners receive any compensation for their labor. You should admire our Führer for his kindness to you."

No one moved a muscle or showed an ounce of emotion.

"Wear shorts and lightweight tops, because the work will be hot. You will get one midday break for soup and water. Any attempt to escape will result in terrible punishment that could make death a welcome relief. Understand?"

We nodded and said, "Yes, sir!"

"Oh, by the way," he said, turning toward us at the barn entrance, "you will not have a day off unless it rains. But, you see, even your God has abandoned you, for it has not rained all summer!" He roared with laughter at the irony of the situation. "You will be issued some rations at 5:00 p.m. Welcome to Camp Barthold, ladies!" With that he gave us the usual Heil Hitler salute and left.

Each of us scrambled to claim a six-foot plot. After Steffi and I grabbed a little area where we could be together, we sprawled out on the prickly straw.

"At least it's not Auschwitz," I told her, "and our heads aren't being shaved." That practice was common at many camps. "Let's praise the Lord for that and pray it rains for forty days and nights. God did that once before. Then we won't have to do that dreadful work."

Steffi smiled faintly.

Some of the women among us were as young as fourteen; a few were in their sixties. How would the older ones endure the hard labor? Would they be worked to death as many others had been in these camps?

We found a short wooden beam in the barn on which we placed

our few belongings. At five o'clock we went into the camp's outer area and lined up for our evening rations. No one had eaten since early morning, and we were all tired and hot from being in the stuffy barn. The thought of doing manual labor in the August heat ten hours a day was almost unthinkable. But hadn't I told Steffi we had a big God who could perform any miracle and who would provide us strength if we only asked?

Our evening meal was just some watery soup with an unknown chunky substance in it. It tasted foul and mysterious, but we ate it anyway. We stood in line with the men. This would be the only time the husbands and wives who had been sent to Barthold together would see one another, except for an occasional evening visit under a guard's watchful eye. Each of us was also given one slice of bread, but we were told that it was our morning ration and that the next meal would not be until noon the following day. Although we all looked longingly at the slice of bread, we knew we must save it for breakfast or we wouldn't be able to endure the long hours of morning labor.

That night we women began to get acquainted with one another. Everyone spoke of the abiding fear they had for loved ones who had been taken away months or years earlier. In many cases they had never heard from those loved ones again. How thankful I was that God had allowed Mother and me to communicate during the last several months. At least I hadn't had to endure a horrible time of waiting and wondering if she was alive (I knew it was just another sign of God's goodness). As I roamed the barn, getting acquainted with the women, I met some of the believers who had come to Christ through Pastor Hornig's ministry.

"I have a Bible," I told them enthusiastically. "We can read it together at night if you like." Many returned a broad smile. Others had become weak in their faith because of life's hardships. Still others would fall away from God at the camp, unable to believe He would allow such an existence. But some would draw even closer to

German troops look on as a group of Jews—all but one of whom are women—dig ditches in a fenced-in lot in Krakow—1939 to 1940. *Courtesy United States Holocaust Memorial Museum*

Him because of Camp Barthold.

The latrine area was wide-open, and it became a frequent place for the guards to amuse themselves since no one had any privacy. Our terrible food rations and questionable diet eventually produced rampant dysentery. However, we were informed that anyone who failed to make it to the latrine on time would be fined a whole month's wages. One brave young man spoke up against such a ridiculous fine. "Even the public toilets in Breslau are only ten cents," he insisted.

The camp roared with laughter. Immediately the SS guard who had issued the warning walked over to him and hit him sharply on the back of the head; all future attempts at lightheartedness in front of the guards were silenced.

At 4:00 a.m. we were jarred from a restless sleep by a harsh voice commanding, "Everyone up! Formation in half an hour!"

Our bodies screamed for more sleep, but they would adjust eventually to our five-hour allotment. I reached for my precious slice of bread and found only rat droppings. Without exception, the rats and other barn creatures had eaten all our morning rations. From then on, we kept our bread tightly sealed in our knapsacks.

After being issued a cup of lukewarm coffee at 5:00 a.m., we marched for an hour to the work area. We found that the men might be marched in a different direction to work, but occasionally we'd work in the same area, even digging the same ditches. This was unspeakable joy for the married couples who could work side by side in the ditches for ten whole hours.

Steffi and I frequently dug together, but the ordeal was almost unbearable for her. She had been far more pampered than I as a child and was not used to such hardship and heartache. Her faith was weaker and her strength was not as great as mine. God gave me an abundance of physical strength, despite my starvation diet of the last seven months.

The work was as relentless as the August sun. We were issued heavy digging equipment, such as shovels or picks, and had to dig up an area until it was nearly six feet deep. If we paused to lean on a shovel and rest, we were threatened or struck by a guard who carried a crudely made weapon that served as a whip. As long as we worked hard and the sweat poured off, we were allowed to talk with our digging partners. We could talk about anything if it was not anti-Hitler;

thus, it provided an opportunity for me to help build up the faith of a stumbling sister or share Christ with an unbeliever. Some of the Jews were completely opposed to the gospel, while others, because of the circumstances, politely listened and asked questions. It was tempting to talk openly about the war or Hitler.

The sweat poured off us in the blazing sun. Shade was unavailable. We virtually ate the dust we stirred up from our digging. Our bodies ached with fatigue by noon, but we still had another four hours of work. After just one day, our hands had huge blisters and our backs were breaking. If a guard turned away for a few moments, we would try to take a break. We lived for the sound of the noon whistle. A horse cart would draw up with buckets of water and equally watery soup. But any liquid was welcome because our thirst was far greater than our hunger. We could rest and talk for half an hour. Steffi and I would sit together and dream of better days.

"Why does God allow this?" Steffi asked that first day. "Why does He allow our people to be slaughtered?"

We leaned back on the parched grass beneath us. "But what about those who live, Steffi? You and I will live to tell our story. I know God weeps when someone dies, especially at the hands of Satan-inspired, power-hungry men." I whispered so the guard wouldn't hear. "I think God cries real tears, as He must have done when Jesus was crucified. All the world turned black because God couldn't look at the sin on the suffering Jesus. But Steffi, He does see us, and He hears the innermost longings of our hearts."

Steffi nodded skeptically.

"You'll see," I said.

The afternoon brought more hours of relentless work. In the future we were sometimes assigned new digging partners, which was an opportunity to make a new friend. Occasionally we could choose any partner; I always made sure to pick Steffi so I could encourage her because her depression seemed to be worsening.

In the late afternoon we lined up and began the long march home. Often we sang German folk songs or marching songs on the way. The guards wanted us to sing songs of the Reich, but we flatly refused and were amazed when we weren't punished. As we marched and sang, curious eyes stared at us from the local farmhouses. I was sure I caught glimpses of compassion on those faces of the people who had been so filled with Nazi propaganda. My feeling would prove to be right, for later the farmers would frequently risk their lives to smuggle us cooked potatoes, vegetables, or buttermilk. They also brought us news of the battlefront if they could pick it up from released announcements or from the faint signal of an underground station in another country. Thus far they could give us few specifics, but we knew for certain that Germany was suffering severe blows that late summer of 1944.

Among the women in the barn were artists, musicians, dancers, and entertainers. Every night we tried to entertain one another some way. The actors put on a pantomime show; the singers wrote songs or sang requests; and the dancers often danced. Some form of entertainment pleased everyone. In the early weeks, conditions were not yet so unbearable that the women would turn against one another; that was around the corner.

I soon knew which women wanted to read the Bible with me, and almost nightly we met in a little huddle at one end of the barn to sing hymns, read the Bible, and pray. We tried to edify and encourage one another, and our group grew from six to ten in less than a week. We would focus on one miracle a day, telling how God had protected us or provided for a need. Each day God performed some small miracle that could be related. More and more the Christians became bold enough to share the gospel of Jesus with their digging partners. God helped them recall whole passages of Scripture they might have memorized years ago; as they shared, it was "instant recall."

Often God filled our stomachs with starvation quantities and gave us refreshed and renewed bodies on only four or five hours of sleep. At our times of greatest despair, a local farmer would relay a message to us that indicated the Allies would soon crush Germany and liberate all prisoners. God seldom let us reach a point of crippling despair, for at just such a time He would send someone who might even have been an angel, to bring us good news or physical nourishment from a farmer's kitchen.

The one thing we prayed for every day was withheld: rain!

For six weeks it didn't rain, so we had no day off. The Nazis delighted in mocking our God, claiming He had little pity on us.

As we marched to work in the predawn haze each morning, I held Steffi's hand firmly, always praying that God would give me the right words to say to her as her skepticism increased.

"We are free compared to some," I said to her one morning. "We don't have barbed wire, and Barthold has no gas chambers."

"The animals in the forest have more than we do," Steffi replied. "At least they have food. Their stomachs don't cry out in pain because they have not eaten."

"They are hunted, and so are we. God has given them speed and us keen minds to outsmart the evil people. You wait and see. God will deliver us, and it will be a miracle."

"He hasn't even given us rain yet," Steffi replied in a defeated manner.

"But His 'angels' brought us buttermilk and boiled eggs last night, Steffi, so today our stomachs aren't crying out in pain."

During August and September, we could bathe in the creek and wash off the caked-on dirt. The swift-flowing creek was glorious—massaging and refreshing our bodies.

We were all getting thin from the hard work and lack of proper food. I lost weight rapidly, although thus far my early childhood training in ballet and athletics had allowed me to maintain my coordination and to work effectively. The painful blisters on my hands turned to calluses, and my body shrank inside my work outfits. The scorching sun had given my skin a leathery, nut-brown consistency and bleached white streaks in my long, blonde hair.

Rudi Wolf was granted permission to walk with me around the camp one evening after supper. He quickened his pace as he saw me waiting for him near the cow barn. His face was alive with hope in the moonlight.

"Anita, I have great news!" he said breathlessly. We walked at a quick pace around the camp area in full view of the guards, talking in hushed tones. But when we approached a guard, we would speak loudly on trivial subjects so as not to arouse suspicion.

"I've always known there was hope, Rudi. What is it?"

"Today, while digging a ditch, I worked on an old farmer's piece of land. He came out of his farmhouse and talked to me as I dug; the guards didn't see him because we were more than six feet in the ground. He told me two families from Berlin are living with him and that civilians are fleeing from the cities to the country because the cities are a big graveyard. Germany is losing the war, and it can't go on much longer!"

We looked over our shoulders to make sure we weren't being followed.

"He said that all during the summer German cities have been leveled by the Allies," Rudi continued. "The Allies are using more high-explosive bombs, which create more damage. As soon as a city makes repairs, the bombs fall again."

"When do you think it will end?"

"Even now the Russians are at the frontiers of the Reich. Rome has been liberated, and other cities too. The war has been lost. The only question that remains is whether it will bring about the complete destruction of Germany. And, Anita, some concentration camps have been liberated! Treblinka and others have been set free by the Russians. It is just a matter of time."

"We must pray, Rudi, that God will be merciful to the German people. They have been the puppets of Hitler, and they have suffered miserably."

"I have bad news, too, Anita." Rudi's face grew rigid and pained, and his eyes watered on the verge of tears. "The old farmer told me that word got out from Auschwitz that six hundred thousand Jews have been gassed in the last few weeks in a last-minute effort to exterminate all the Jews there. Adolf Eichmann finally has admitted to Germany that six million Jews have been killed thus far by the Reich, for which Hitler said the world will be eternally grateful."

I couldn't respond. Rudi and I walked in silence. Someday the world would know.

A few minutes later, I cleared the great lump in my throat. "Did the farmer have news about Theresienstadt?" I questioned fearfully.

"No, but I think the Russians are moving closer to it."

Quick-stepping footsteps behind us grew louder, and soon a long rifle appeared between Rudi and me. "That's enough. Go back to the cow barn, kid," the SS man barked at me.

I both rejoiced and grieved over Rudi's news. The "glorious" days of the Reich were coming to an end.

Monotonous days rolled into weeks at the camp. Our bread rations decreased, and our soup rations grew more foul. My stomach, weakened by the severe attack of jaundice over a year ago, rebelled against the diet; I could eat very little. Although I continued to lose weight, my heavenly Father gave me enough strength to carry on with the work schedule without drawing undue attention from the guards. Others suffered more from heat exhaustion; it was the hottest, driest summer and fall in German history. My heart went out to those who collapsed daily in the mid-afternoon sun. They were given little mercy or relief. A pail of water might be dumped over them, followed by a stern lecture on the strength of the pure Aryan race and the weakness of us despicable Jews. With that, a pick was forced back in their hands and a gun butt drove them back into the trenches.

The unending days and short nights were bearable for us believers because we could edify each other. I knew all of the women who professed faith in Christ, but I was unsure of the men. One mid-September day, when the scorching summer sun had finally eased up, I was assigned to dig with Gunther Czech. His nineteen-year-old face was radiant with a beauty that sprang from an inner source. Within a few moments, we identified each other as Jewish believers in Jesus. How we gloried in our discovery! We hardly noticed the heavy clay soil we pitched that day because our spirits were in such harmony. What's more, our mothers knew one another.

"Gunther, your mother's name is Hilde, just like my mother's. Mother used to talk to me about Hilde Czech. She was so happy to meet another Jewish woman who believed in Jesus."

"Come to think of it," Gunther said, "my mother mentioned the name of Hilde Dittman." Gunther didn't break his digging stride, and the sweat poured down our faces even on this relatively cool day.

"What happened to your mother, Gunther?"

"She's in Theresienstadt."

"Gunther, so is mine!"

Gunther gave me a broad smile. "Anita, if we ever get out of here, we'll meet again in Theresienstadt when we go to find our mothers. Perhaps we can even go together."

As I marched home that afternoon, I felt glorious. It seemed that I was always encouraging someone, giving of myself until I felt almost dried up. Today Gunther had refreshed and replenished me. God had known and had sent me a new friend. Whatever my need, God provided.

As Steffi's body adjusted to the grind, she began to lose some of her depression. She found a few new friends who were interested in the theater as she was, but she drifted from talk about God, which disappointed me. I saw her smile occasionally or even laugh, and she cried less and less.

The women's prayer group increased as others saw that something fortified and strengthened those of us who met to pray together. Many came once out of curiosity but never came back. Others came and were offended at all the talk about Jesus. Some sat back and cautiously observed us; later, in the trenches, they asked me questions about Jesus, about being Jewish and believing in Jesus, and about heaven and hell. To them, hell was life on earth. Many of the curious women couldn't figure out why we Christians weren't seething with bitter hatred for the Nazis and why we didn't curse the world for caring so little about our plight. At first they came one by one with skeptical questions. Then they came two by two, and later by the half dozen. So many questions. So many quick answers needed. Jesus, I prayed silently, *Speak through me. Let me live what I say!*

After six weeks of continuous labor, we were given a delightful treat: We could each make one phone call to a relative and invite him or her to visit us. I was sure all my relatives on Mother's side were now either killed or in the camps; that left only Father to call. Nevertheless, I looked forward to the call, savoring the thought of it all day.

Finally, it was my turn to go into the main building and use the phone. I dialed Father's number as other prisoners lined up behind me. Father didn't know I'd been taken to a camp. How would he act? Apathetic? Shocked? Oh, he had to sound mortified, or I would be so terribly hurt. *Thank You, Jesus,* I prayed, *that I have a heavenly Father to comfort me when an earthly one fails.*

I dialed the outdated country phone and waited until I heard Father's familiar voice.

"Hi, Dad," I said enthusiastically.

"Anita! Where are you? Someone said you were on one of the last trainloads sent to a camp from Breslau. Is it true?"

"Yes, Dad. I'm at Barthold near Schmiegrode. I can't talk long now, but I can have a visitor next Saturday. Would you come and see me?"

"Yes. Can I bring some food?" he inquired.

"Yes, that would be good. About twenty people are waiting to use the phone, so I'll say good-bye now. Dad, I miss you."

I waited for several long seconds for a reply.

"Anita, I'm sorry this has happened. I am so sorry."

"It was good hearing your voice, Dad. Good-bye. God bless." The last two words didn't penetrate his atheistic bitterness, I knew.

That night the cow barn was alive with expectation and an excitement that had to be shared. A week from now almost everyone would have a visitor. Our talk was animated as we sat on the straw-covered floor. Steffi and I talked long after the others had fallen asleep. She would be visited by her father, whom she loved very much. At last everyone had something to live for.

* * *

Our eyes met, but for an instant Father didn't recognize me. Instead, he kept moving to look for me elsewhere. Then a sad realization came over his face, and he came back to me. I saw great compassion in his cold eyes as he looked at my thin body and gaunt face. When I smiled at him, Father came over and embraced me. It had taken this tragedy to bridge the enormous gap that had existed between us all those years.

"I've missed you," he said, his voice cracking with emotion.

"I'm okay, Dad. I've lived for this all week."

Father lifted a knapsack off his back and opened it. "I've brought you some food, Anita. Look—apples, pears, some pudding, red cabbage, and potato dumplings. I even brought some cold chicken."

It looked delicious! I motioned for Father to follow me as we headed for a patch of weeds near the cow barn. As we walked, he scanned the camp's bleak conditions—conditions fit for barnyard animals but not humans. Finally, his flashing eyes looked only at me. Reaching the spot where we could sit and visit, Father spread out his coat for us to sit on. He was doing his best to ease the awkwardness of our reunion.

Emptying the knapsack, he set all the food before me in neat little stacks. "I'd forgotten that such food exists!" I exclaimed. "I'm not sure I can eat it all. You won't be offended, will you?"

Dad shook his head.

I glanced around the camp area and saw the other prisoners with their visitors scattered all over the meadows. They hovered over one another in small clusters. Armed guards were posted everywhere, keeping a watchful eye. We all kept our voices low, with a minimum amount of expression on our faces.

I ate the pudding and dumplings, but almost immediately, I felt terrible stomach cramps. Not wanting to let Father see that I was in agony, I forced a faint smile. The pain came in horrible, wrenching spasms. After existing for so long on a starvation diet, my whole system was overreacting to normal, nourishing food.

"Germany is finished, isn't she, Dad?" I asked. "We've heard Hitler is crushed. My friend Rudi Wolf says that we should hear the Russian guns of liberation in the distance anytime."

"Yes, Germany has taken a terrible beating. Our cities are ruined. I heard an estimate that half a million German civilians have been killed in the air raids. The Allies are closing in on all fronts, so it is just a matter of time. But it is very difficult to get accurate information. The Nazis don't paint us a realistic picture, you know.

"What about Theresienstadt? I've heard some of the camps have been liberated."

"A few in the East have, as the Russians advance, but I don't think Theresienstadt has been liberated yet."

My awful bitterness toward Father welled up again. If he had not deserted us, perhaps Mother and I wouldn't be rotting in these camps. Yet, I decided, it must be God's will for us to be in them, for we could share our faith in Jesus with other prisoners. Therefore, Father's rejection of us was also in God's plan, and I knew I should not be overly hard on him.

"Tell me about camp life," he said.

I didn't paint the grim picture I could have, but my physical appearance indicated some of the severity of the situation.

"It's all right, Dad. At least Hella got out in time. She never could have endured Nazi Germany, you know. Mother and I have our faith, but she had none. I'm able to encourage a lot of people here at Barthold. They ask me about Jesus and—"

"Enough of that, Anita. You know I can't believe it."

"But I'm living proof of a God, Dad."

"Stop it."

Footsteps in the grass a few yards away told us our time was about to end. We'd visited nearly an hour, but now the guards had begun to send the visitors home. After Father put the empty knapsack on his back, he embraced me again. Then he turned and walked away. After a few yards, he turned back to me.

"I'll come again, Anita, if they will let me." He waved, and then I watched him disappear out the camp entrance and down a winding road toward the railroad. The visits had brought as much agony as they had pleasure for us prisoners. The good-byes were unbearable, and now we had only memories again. The day held the gamut of human emotion: indescribable joy of reunion and then heartrending tears of separation.

11

SUSTAINED

With the onset of the cool weather, we lost our bathing spot in the creek. Now we bathed with water from a round, twelve-inch enamel basin shared by ten women. We had a rigid schedule so that everyone had enough time to get clean, but under those conditions, no one did a very good job. As things grew worse, most of us contracted head lice. The crawling, itching bugs were eager to make homes in our hair, causing the utmost agony when they succeeded. They multiplied alarmingly, and the sensation of dozens of them crawling over our heads nearly drove us crazy.

For days we were given no medication. Finally, when we nearly rioted, we were given medicine that not only killed the lice but also removed much of our hair.

Late one afternoon, we were all transported to a nearby village that had a large, public bathing place. For ten whole minutes we were allowed a hot bath. It was pure luxury. As I gazed at myself in the bathhouse mirror, I did a double take. My cheeks were sunken and hollow, and my eyes were set deep within my face. The lice medicine on my head had caused huge patches of my hair to fall out, leaving giant bald spots. The sun had baked my skin to a dark brown shade, and it was dry and peeling. At seventeen I was an old woman.

October brought rain, but the men in charge changed their minds about giving us a day off and made us dig ditches in the mud. Since we had no facilities to dry our work clothes, we simply wore them wet the next day.

As conditions worsened—the horrible lack of food, the unending labor, the unsanitary living quarters, and the increased security measures—everyone's spirits tumbled, and the women became less tolerant of one another. For some, even their faith in God weakened; I knew God wanted me to strengthen their faith. My little torn and mud-stained Bible had been handled by so many dirty hands that its pages were hardly readable. I knew the guards had seen the Bible, but they had not taken it away.

Apparently because some of us had one Aryan parent, and many of us were believers in Christ, we were treated less harshly. Our brothers and sisters in Bergen-Belsen, Buchenwald, Treblinka, Auschwitz, and other camps huddled behind barbed-wire fences, were used as medical guinea pigs, tortured for an afternoon's amusement, and ultimately murdered in a variety of vicious ways. By comparison, we lived in a children's play world. And yet rumor had it that when our ditch-digging assignment was completed, we were to be gassed or shot like our brothers and sisters in the other camps.

Our entire camp was moved northwest to another area, near the village of Ostlinde, in November 1944. The vast ditches that we dug (so the German army could trap the advancing Russian tanks) were left behind, and so were the kind farmers who had helped us in many little ways. Our ranks at Barthold had increased over the last few months, as new prisoners were added almost weekly. There were five hundred of us when we marched out of Barthold and down the country road to the railroad station. The kind farmers peered out of their windows and bravely waved good-bye. War wasn't even in their backyard, but their eyes said they had seen enough.

When we reached the new camp, we were made to stand

outside in formation while the cold wind tore through our simple cotton clothes. A harsh, bulldog-looking man was our new camp leader. Mr. Anders was a brutal SS man who snarled angry commands at us as we stood there shivering.

Life was about the same at the new camp, but now we had to contend with the winter elements and much more crowded conditions. The women were divided into two groups of about one hundred, each group occupying a moderate-sized wooden structure heated by one tiny, wood-burning stove. Our beds were simply gunnysacks filled with straw—just a step above a barn floor. At least we had outhouses rather than an open latrine.

All the men were jammed into one building called 'the fort." Their living conditions were similar, but they were much more crowded.

Again we marched off to work at 5:00 a.m., but now we were accompanied by the piercing cold. Our assignment was to cut down giant pine trees. We stripped the trees of their branches and then wrapped the branches around the trunk and wired them together. After the strange contraptions were stacked in orderly piles, horse carts transported them to the tank traps we had dug earlier. There they were used to reinforce the walls of the pits to keep the soil from sliding down. Fortunately, our bodies warmed up as we worked. Again, it was monotonous but bearable because we could work with a friend of like faith. God blessed me so richly with friends. I had Steffi, Gunther, Ruth, Gerhard, and another dozen or so strong believers in Jesus. We met for prayer as often as possible. Sometimes we just huddled together in the cold as we held hands and prayed. Depending on their whim at the moment, the guards would break us up angrily, while at other times they stood at a distance and mocked us. Our ranks grew to about twenty strong believers in Jesus. We prayed for the German people and for Germany—that God would spare the innocent victims of the war and that He would restore the Fatherland in spite of the Führer's attempt at genocide against all non-Aryans.

Rudi's words seldom left my mind; "Any day we should hear the Russian guns of liberation." I listened and listened. During an early November thunderstorm, my heart raced with anticipation, for I was sure the thunderclaps were Russian guns firing in the distance.

By now I had lost over twenty pounds, and often when one of the women would scrub my back, she would say, "Anita, it's like scrubbing an old washboard!" I resembled a brown-skinned Indian about to become a skeleton. I grew weaker and noticed I could hardly climb the stairs to our living quarters each night after work.

Almost daily, my symptoms worsened; Steffi, Gunther, and the Wolf brothers were worried about me. Others looked angrily at me because I could no longer work as fast as they. Consequently they feared they were doing some of my work. I knew my symptoms had slowed me down so much that I probably appeared to be a lazy worker.

For days I wrestled with the only alternative: to report myself to Mr. Anders, who would send me to sick bay, a tiny country hospital run by the Nazis in Ostlinde. I seriously doubted that the Nazi doctors and nurses would care if they helped an ailing prisoner. All the Nazi hospitals had clever methods for the "elimination of undesirables." If prisoners could not contribute to the function of the work camps, the doctors would simply kill them by withholding necessary medicine or administering death-inducing drugs. Yet, as the pains increased and I grew weaker, I realized I must take the chance and put my life completely in God's hands. If He wanted me to survive this brutal war, He could work out the details and have the medical staff see some worth in me.

The next morning I sat nervously in a tiny room at the hospital as I waited for the doctor to examine me. The hospital was an interesting combination of the old world and the new, with its outdated telephone and hospital furniture surrounded by modern medical science. I could hardly sit up straight for the pains. I wasn't sure if the physical pain or the emotional tension was worse as I waited. Three days without food had also weakened me. Finally an angry-looking Nazi doctor shuffled through the door. He was tall, blonde, and handsome. Surely he was what Nazism and the "pure race" were all about. The door slammed behind him, and he stood over me in a defiant manner.

"So you've lost twenty pounds; is that right?" He scowled.

"Yes, sir."

"So what if you've lost weight?" he replied. "I've lost some too. It is a small sacrifice for the Fatherland and for the Führer. Some beds are in the hall. Go there and lie down. We will keep you here a few days and give you some medicine. I am told you are needed to cut trees, so your stay will be brief. If you don't recover quickly—well, we'll see about that if the time comes."

I was suspicious because he didn't even examine me. Maybe I had already been written off as dead, and they would simply finalize the act. Leaving the room, I walked toward the small hospital ward area. There I saw ten little beds with mattresses and blankets. Such luxury! Most of the beds were empty, but I saw a thin girl stir on one of them. As she lifted her head, I recognized Ann Czech, Gunther's sister, also a believer. How good God was to provide a fellow Christian for me in the hospital!

"Anita! What are you doing here?"

I went over and sat on the edge of the bed next to Ann. "I've had terrible stomach pains, and I'm weak and dizzy."

"Anita, you must be very careful here. Many prisoners don't leave this hospital because they are killed by the staff."

"I know."

"Have you eaten?"

"I haven't eaten in three days because of these terrible pains."

"Let's pray right now, Anita, for your pains. Let's ask God to heal you so you won't have to take their poison."

We had prayed only a few minutes before we heard footsteps. I changed into a scanty hospital gown and climbed into bed. How wonderful it was to lie in a real bed with blankets and a feather pillow.

"They feed me only potatoes," Ann said. "I will share them with you because you might be starved to death here. You look like a walking skeleton. You must eat the starchy potatoes even if your pains persist. If you get any thinner, the Nazis will have no need for you because you won't be able to work. Promise you'll eat some of my potatoes."

"I promise."

A Nazi nurse walked in and stood by my bed. In her hand she held a glass of water and a little cup with a yellow pill in it. "You are to take these little yellow pills three times a day, Miss Dittman," she said. "They will help you regain your strength more quickly. Take this one now while I watch you."

She stood over me with her arms folded and gazed down at me. I plopped the pill in my mouth and washed it down with the good-tasting well water. Then a pleased look came over her face, and she turned and left.

"Anita!" Ann howled after the nurse left. "Don't take those pills! You don't know what they are. They could kill you slowly or weaken or poison you. Why didn't you listen to me when I warned you?"

"But what was I to do? She stood over me."

"Next time, put it in your mouth and pretend to swallow it. Then spit out the pill when she leaves."

Ann was right. A half hour later I began to vomit. Indeed, the pill was intended to weaken me more in order to kill me. I was too thin to be of any use to the Reich any longer. Since my stomach was empty, I had the dry heaves. The nurse had a look of sweet satisfaction as she put a bucket by my bed.

Later that evening, I was brought some watery soup and another little yellow pill. Just as Ann instructed, I placed the pill in my mouth and pretended to swallow it eagerly. Then I pushed around my watery soup as the nurse left. Ann fed me half of her potato meal that night and at every meal for the next few days. I ate the potato rations under the covers so the staff wouldn't see. Then I'd run to the outdoor bathroom and make terrible sounds as though I was vomiting from the pills.

Six days later I had gained six pounds and felt strong again! The staff looked at me in amazement. Ann, who had been admitted because of painful arthritis, could bend her joints with little pain now. God had truly performed a miracle by restoring our strength and health, which allowed us to leave the Nazi death hospital. Bewildered, the hospital staff called a guard to escort us back to the work camp; once there, we were ordered to resume hard labor immediately.

We prayed that God would miraculously sustain our strength; each day our food rations diminished so the German soldiers on the battlefronts could receive more food. Shortly after all of us Christians had prayed for physical strength, the neighboring farmers again rallied for us. Risking their lives, they smuggled us sausage, bread, and cheese and told us to eat the nourishing mushrooms in the forest where we cut trees. God seemed to pack a thousand calories in each tiny mushroom and bite of bread as we who trusted Jesus were given physical and spiritual sustenance.

Two horrible realities faced us women in December: winter and the traitors among us. To make life more comfortable for themselves, some women were reporting others to the guards for such things as conversations, attitudes, or anti-Nazi sentiment—anything that would make their lives more comfortable. Many of them spent the night with the guards and were given preferential treatment.

As the winter winds increased, everyone's spirits sank. Our uniforms were terribly inadequate, and many of us were sent clothes from home. Father sent me some warm socks, gloves, and a jacket. If we worked long enough and hard enough, we could keep ourselves relatively warm on the work line. But marching to and from the work area was difficult because the wind raced through our clothing. Again we anxiously awaited the whistle when the horse cart would bring us warm, lumpy soup. But it tasted awful, and usually it was cold by the time it reached us. The chunks in the soup were like tree bark. I watched Gunther one day as he took his bowl of soup to a mock grave. Pouring the soup in the grave, he covered it with dirt. Then he took a large stone and placed it over the grave site. On the stone he wrote: *"Hier ruhet still una unvergessen, unser heutiges Mittagessen."* ("Here rests, still and unforgotten, today's menu.")

Just before Christmas I met another beautiful believer: Christian Risel. We met on the work line while cutting trees and, in our own silent way, quickly fell in love. Though I loved Rudi, Wolfgang, Gerhard, and Gunther, the love in my heart for Christian was different. A little older than I, he was strong and handsome in spite of the months of labor and deprivation. His eyes virtually sparkled, while the eyes of others in the camp were glassy and dazed. He had a smile when everyone else had a negative word, for he loved everyone in a special way. He even had Christian compassion for the Nazis. But he loved me the most. Of course no time was allowed for romance in the camp. It was too cold to stay outside much in our thin clothing, and we couldn't go inside each other's quarters. But we cut trees together frequently and got to know one another better. Each day that we were together, our love was reaffirmed.

"Someday, Anita, we will be gloriously free and happy once again," Christian said as his axe cut into a thick pine tree. "We will have money to spend and food to eat, and we will have loved ones surrounding us. We'll never have to dread another knock on our door. Do you believe that too, Anita?"

"I do. God reaffirms it every day. But I would rather be locked away and have Jesus than to be my sister, Hella, safe in the free world but denying the very One who gave her freedom."

"Nothing happens without a purpose, does it?" Christian said. "What do you suppose is our ultimate purpose for being trapped in Nazi Germany? I think it is to glorify God in the end. Do you think that is true?"

"I do, Christian."

"Anita, do you know what day it is today?"

"No."

"It is Christmas Eve. I have a surprise for you and the other Christians in the camp."

"Why have you waited so long to tell me, Christian?"

"Because it was just confirmed at lunchtime." Christian's eyes really sparkled with excitement now. "Mr. Anders has given me permission to take all the Christians to a Christmas Eve service in Ostlinde tonight! Of course, a guard will accompany us, but he will be exposed to the gospel too."

"Christian, you don't mean it! A real Christmas Eve service! We must spread the news!. Oh, it is another miracle of God!"

To war-weary Christian prisoners who loved Jesus, this was the best news in months, perhaps years. But the camp's unbelievers had no time for our happiness; most of them felt no special comfort each day, as we believers did. Whether they were jealous or skeptical, they preferred that we keep to ourselves, which only drew us closer together.

Twenty of us trudged over the snow-covered hills and meadows that night to a little country church at the edge of Ostlinde. The snow was falling lightly, and both melted snowflakes and tears dampened my face as Christian took my hand.

"This will be the most meaningful Christmas I've ever had," I told him. "It shows God's very special love for us. It tells me He cares for us and that we'll be all right in the end."

"The birth of Jesus must have been like this," Christian said quietly. "He was poor and persecuted, and He was misunderstood and rejected, yet He always forgave. We have to forgive too, Anita, even the Nazis."

That night we huddled in the little church with a hundred or more of the farmers and townspeople. We sang Christmas carols and praised the Lord until well after midnight. As we read the Christmas story, we were reassured that Jesus knew our every ache because He also had been a man and had experienced human grief. In the dim candlelight we all gathered at the altar on our knees and prayed for Germany and our separated families; the guard stood careful watch in the doorway.

Then we trudged home in the moonlight, for the snow had stopped falling. No one spoke a word; we all were savoring every minute of this blessed Christmas Eve.

"The villagers say that the Russians are nearly on German soil," Christian said to me one day in January 1945 as we marched home from the work area. "They say that Auschwitz has been liberated by the Russians!"

"Praise God!" The horror stories that came from Auschwitz and Dachau were always unbelievable. Theresienstadt also would score high on the horror scale, but fortunately I didn't know that, and my hope lived on that Mother was well.

"I was told we were all headed for the gas chambers in Auschwitz," Christian said, "as soon as our work was finished here. It came from a reliable source, so I think it's true. The Russians may advocate godless Communism, Anita, but they are setting our people free. God's ways are strange, aren't they?"

Daily we watched the Ostlinde villagers flee further west to escape the advancing Russians. First the women and children went, then the others. Ostlinde was quickly becoming a ghost town, which gave us renewed hope of freedom.

In spite of this precarious situation, we were allowed visitors one more time. I got word to Father, who had promised to come the next time visitors were allowed. This time I would be able to eat all the precious food he might bring because God had restored my stomach and eased the terrible pains. The camp grew alive with expectation again as we anticipated the visitors' day. We scrubbed ourselves for an hour with soap, which was nothing but clay. Despite our troubles, a light spirit fell on the camp. Perhaps our most difficult daily ordeal was never having anything to look forward to. Suddenly nearly everyone could anticipate a visitor, and that anticipation swept through the camp like a bracing wind.

A few skeptics thought it was just a trick, a prank. Maybe the visitors would be hauled off to prisons, too, as soon as the Nazis found out who they were. The pessimistic rumor was not all that far-fetched.

Father looked weary when I saw him enter the camp's main area. We met indoors in a lounge area normally used by guards. Our visit was limited to about fifteen minutes so that other visitors could then use the lounge.

"Anita, you look so much better," he said as we met.

"Jesus has helped me regain my strength."

"That's nonsense," Father replied. "Please keep such talk to yourself, Anita, because I do not want to waste our time."

For a flash I saw the father I always knew—angry, bitter, and trying to make it through life without God, even in the hell of Germany.

"Do you know anything of Mother?" I asked. "Has any news come out of Theresienstadt?"

"The only news is bad news. I'm told Theresienstadt is a pitiful death camp. I don't want to discourage you, Anita, but you should know the truth. Theresienstadt, Auschwitz, and Dachau are reported to be the worst. Of course, Auschwitz has been liberated, but not the others. The camps that are filled with Orthodox and other religious Jews are getting the brunt of Eichmann's assault.

That includes Theresienstadt. But don't be in total despair; a few will make it. Your mother is strong, Anita."

"Isn't the war nearly over, Dad?"

"The British and the Americans have blown our cities out of existence. Everywhere Germans are struggling in hopeless confusion. A few have hung out white flags, but they have been seriously punished. Warsaw will probably fall to the Russians any day. It is sad, Anita. Perhaps those of you in the camps are really the ones that are free. Bombs don't fall on you, and the Allies are trying to free you."

God was indeed judging the German people for their blind devotion to Hitler, their shameless peddler of lies, deceit, demagoguery, and anti-Semitism. That devotion allowed a reign of terror on Europe and Russia that was felt around the world. Now it was Germany's turn to plead for mercy.

How I wanted Father to escape the coming siege. More than that, I wanted him to know Jesus so that ultimately it wouldn't matter if we lived or died in this massive German graveyard. I wanted him to have the same ultimate and glorious future that Mother and I had waiting for us—an eternity of reunions with lost loved ones, sitting at the throne of the One who made it possible. The aching in my heart over Father's spiritual emptiness increased as he gently kissed me good-bye on the forehead that afternoon. As he grew smaller in the distance, I had a sinking feeling I would never see him again.

Frigid January temperatures were painful as we marched to the work area each morning in the dark. The snow-covered roads were slippery under our wooden shoes. Our mittens were worn thin from the long hours of hard labor; freezing fingers made wiring the pine branches around the tree trunks a painful process.

Christian and I grew more in love; it is amazing what the body can endure when it has that security. God always was so good to me that I felt like the luckiest woman in the camp.

Christian, who had an incredible way with Mr. Anders, got his permission to use the little country church for a classical concert. Christian, who played the violin, planned the entire performance. I'll never know where the performers found their instruments: a flute, a viola, a trumpet, a cello, and two violins. The tiny church organ was used too. The church was dark and unheated, the only light coming from the organ loft above the pews. About ten musicians squinted in the dim light to see the music Christian had written for them. Nearly a hundred classical-music lovers from the camp, accompanied by armed guards, came to the church. Bundled up with blankets to keep warm in the near-zero temperatures, we squeezed close together so we could share our body heat.

It was glorious to become lost in the beautiful world of Handel, Mozart, and Bach. Just as on Christmas Eve, we forgot about our growling stomachs and the bitter cold.

And like Christmas Eve, as we headed back to the camp over the snowdrifts, in the stillness of that dark, dark night, nobody spoke. Our silent communication conveyed a oneness that superseded all verbal expression.

Saturated with the restful music and with gratitude to God, I sank into a deep and restful sleep on my straw mattress.

12

a taste of freedom

Our camp leaders suddenly ordered us to pack our things one evening in late January and be in formation by 9:30 p.m. An evening formation was unusual. It was a cold, stormy night, and the sky refused to let the moon and stars lend us any light. Confusion was everywhere, even among Mr. Anders and the guards. The remaining farmers and villagers of Ostlinde had scurried away from the town that night. Obviously the Russians were advancing quickly and would soon be in Ostlinde. As a result we were to be marched on foot to some unknown destination. Would it be a place of execution? I grabbed Christian's hand as we waited in the unorganized formation.

"Christian, we could escape in all this confusion!" I whispered. "They would never see us or find out. The train comes through Ostlinde later tonight and goes straight to Breslau."

"No!" Christian insisted as he tugged at my hand. "It's not safe. Stay right here with me."

How I thank God I listened to Christian, for later I learned that a dozen prisoners who did flee in such a manner that night were caught at the Breslau train station. The Gestapo dragged them to a vacant house and held them there for days. My dear friends the Wolf brothers were among them. Later a bomb was deliberately dropped on the house by the Gestapo—a terrifying example of what could happen to prisoners who tried to escape.

A few others who escaped that night hid in the village of Ostlinde. When the Russians invaded the town, the prisoners were mistaken for German ambush troops and were arrested and sent to Siberian prison camps. Since we were never given prison identification to defend ourselves against such a situation, the Russians didn't believe the hiding prisoners.

All night long we marched without boots through deep snow. Our small suitcases and knapsacks felt as if they had turned to lead. And our brisk pace could not ward off the cold. While we marched, we weren't allowed to talk, though Christian was at my side, and we had established some nonverbal communication. Just his presence was good enough for me.

Our bodies ached for rest and warmth and food. Coupled with the physical discomforts was the confusion. What was happening, and where were we going? To our execution? By the Germans, or by the Russians? The night seemed endless. We pressed forward without a break or altering our pace. Uncertainty reigned. Women wept. Some dropped from exhaustion, but we didn't stop. As we walked through mounds of snow, our thin wooden shoes filled with snow, deadening our feet with cold. Would it never end? Were we being marched to death just as German prisoners of war were marched to death in Russia? Only a great big God who loved me so much could put peace in my heart during this ordeal.

A faint glimmer of dawn appeared on the eastern horizon, and we estimated it must be about 6:30 a.m. Shortly afterward we came to another little village, and we finally were allowed to rest for a few moments near the center of town. A thick forest lay just a few yards from us, and we could see the first rays of sunrise begin to peek through the thick pines. Christian, with his sister, Hilde, Hella Frommelt, and I sat together and breathed deeply, trying to catch our breath from the eight-hour walk. All the guards gathered for a conference, turning their backs on the prisoners for a moment.

"Christian, we could flee to the woods right now!" I whispered. "Look, they're not watching us."

Fatigue, exhaustion, cold, and hunger numbed all of our brains. Christian thought for a few seconds. Finally, he nodded his approval and signaled Hilde, Hella, and me to follow him in a quick dash to the woods. It was still dark enough to make it. In another few minutes the dawn would reveal our plan. We had to move now.

Swift as gazelles, we bounded into the woods, turning on a burst of speed none of us thought we had left. Several prisoners saw our escape; we were at their mercy to keep quiet.

We pushed through the thick layer of snow as branches and twigs cut our faces, our ankles twisting as we fell into holes and crashed into trees in the predawn darkness. A dozen times Christian broke his stride to pick us up out of the snow. My throat grew raw and cold from gasping at the cold air, and my heart was racing so hard with fear and exhaustion that I thought it would stop beating at any moment. I listened for four consecutive gunshots that would stop us all, but they never came.

"Hilde and Hella can't keep up," I panted to Christian, who led the pack. "They are falling behind. We must help them."

Christian paused and balanced himself against a tree limb, trying to catch his breath. I fell to the ground to rest. In a moment, we heard the crunching sound of footsteps in the snow as Hilde and Hella caught up with us. From the cold and the exercise, their faces glowed like red lightbulbs in the dim light of dawn.

"We must rest," Hella pleaded. "We can't go on."

"But we must go on," Christian replied. "I can see moving lights ahead. I think it's a road. God will give us the strength."

In some places the snow was knee-deep. Now and then a curious squirrel or a rabbit would look at us in confusion, having no idea how lucky it was to live in a tranquil world.

We heard an engine rumble and saw more moving lights. It had to be a road just ahead. Perhaps more fleeing Germans were on the run to escape the Russians. We pushed ahead, not looking back, and finally reached the edge of the forest. Below us lay an unpaved road. Coming down the bumpy road was an old, empty dump truck being driven by a bearded German. Christian ran to the middle of the road and waved, and the old man stopped. He stuck his rugged face out the window.

"Hop on!" he said without asking any questions. "I'm heading several kilometers west. We're trying to keep ahead of the Russians. My family left last week."

We climbed on the back of the truck and sat on some cement bags that lined the truck. Our thin bodies ached every time the old man hit a bump and we came down hard on the bags.

"Pray hard," I said. "Pray that we don't drive right into Mr. Anders and the others." Since we were turned around, we had no idea which way we were going in relation to the marching prisoners.

We were too exhausted to talk as the putrid exhaust came out of the tailpipe and drifted up to us. I sat as close as I could to Christian, and he put his arm around me. In spite of the cold, the hunger, and the bumpy ride, I drifted off to sleep on Christian's shoulder. But then reality would jar me awake within seconds. Alertness was a must, and we all felt as though we were riding shotgun on a stage-coach going west, about to be attacked by Indians. We had read about such American history in our school textbooks.

About an hour later we came to a deserted little village. We quietly hopped off the truck so the old man would not know when we left, for no one could really be trusted in Germany. He could have been taking us straight to the Gestapo.

The little village had an aura of panic about it. Even in the dead of winter, front doors had been left open and house lights burning.

We cautiously peeked into some deserted houses; in one house, embers still burned in a fireplace. Some of the town's residents must have fled only hours earlier; others remained but looked cautiously out of windows.

We entered the empty house with the dying fire. It was still warm and cozy, even though many household items were missing, evidently taken by fleeing owners.

"I'll get some logs and stoke up the fire," Christian said. "Anita, see if they've left any food."

Hilde and Hella collapsed in front of the fireplace as I made my way into the kitchen. While Christian searched for firewood, I went through every cupboard in an attempt to find a morsel of food. God provided, for I stumbled across some smoked bacon, bread, noodles, and a bag of peas and lentils. Even a small bag of tea had been left behind. With such a combination I would be able to make a gourmet meal for the four of us!

We huddled by the fire and ate our meal as the morning sun smiled at us through the windows. Because of our hunger, we ate quickly and didn't speak for at least ten minutes. We could hear only the crackling fire and the exuberant birds as they welcomed the new day in the peaceful village. Evidently the villagers had gotten word of the advancing Russians, but some had chosen to stay behind and take their chances. Though we were riddled with curiosity and questions, we didn't dare venture out into the street and be seen. A town that size would easily spot an outsider.

"What do we do next?" I questioned Christian as we finished eating.

"I don't know. We could wait for the Russians, but we have no identification to prove we're prisoners. We have only our work clothes, and they probably aren't distinctive enough to convince them that we're not the enemy."

"Why don't we try to make it to Breslau?" Hella asked.

"For now I think we'll stay right here," Christian said. "We'll think and pray about what we should do. I don't think God would lead us into danger. Who knows? The war might end tomorrow."

It seemed that Christian always knew just what to do and how to do it. He had a way about him that made us feel absolutely confident and safe around him. We were sure that his judgment was correct and unquestionable.

All that day we rested in the abandoned home but kept one ear open to the sound of marching feet. For all we knew, Mr. Anders and the whole band of prisoners could be marching through the town. It would not surprise us if Mr. Anders sent out a team of guards to round us up, now that they would have noticed we were missing. We also listened carefully for the sound of Russian guns in the distance, for under the circumstances our lives could be in great danger from the Russians. We had always thanked God that concentration camp numbers had not been painfully burned onto our arms; on the other hand, that would definitely identify us as war victims.

Even before the sun set that day, we had drifted into restful sleep in front of the fireplace. We had been up the whole previous night, and we had chattered away the day with hopeful expectations and dreams of our free lives. Our bodies ached from the long march to outrun both the Nazis and Russians. Though I thanked God for our freedom, thoughts still annoyed me about the safety of Steffi, Gunther, Ann, and other precious friends and believers left behind. Were they being taken to a camp that had a gas chamber? Though freedom was an obsession to us all, I wasn't so sure I could enjoy it as long as my friends' fate was in question.

Stabbing hunger pains awakened us early the next morning. Our delicious meal from the day before was completely gone; all that remained was some weak tea that we warmed up. Obviously we had no ration cards to obtain any food in the tiny town. We tried to suppress our hunger as the day wore on. We sat by the fire again and thanked God for more than twenty-four hours of freedom.

"Surely we are safe now," I said confidently to the others as Christian tossed another log in the fireplace. My confidence sounded almost arrogant.

"We can't be sure," Christian said. "It would seem so, but a lot can still happen, you know."

"But Anders and the others would have marched through here hours ago," Hilde insisted.

"Perhaps," Christian answered cautiously. He peered carefully out the front window. "It's a sleepy little town that remains. Since we're staying here for a little while, I'm going to risk going out to find some food."

"Christian!" I protested.

"I must, Anita. We will starve here eventually, and it won't get any safer in the next week. The three of you pray as I try to find something for us to eat."

"Christian, I'm going with you," I said. "You must let me come along."

"No, I insist that you stay behind. Why should more than one of us get caught?"

"But they will know you're a prisoner," I pleaded. "All young men are either soldiers or prisoners."

"I will take the chance."

"At least wait until dark, Christian," I said.

Christian didn't wait to reply but walked out of the house as he buttoned his jacket. Hilde, Hella, and I paced nervously and prayed intermittently that God would protect Christian as he roamed like a moving target throughout the little town.

"If anyone can handle this situation, it is Christian," his sister, Hilde, said proudly. "He will know exactly what to do."

Hella nodded her head in agreement, and suddenly I felt as if I were a silly mother hen. I peeked out the window to survey the situation, but Christian was nowhere to be seen. I didn't even know his plan of action—whether he was truly hoping to find food in another abandoned house or actually planning to approach someone who might offer food without questions.

Nearly half an hour passed as we waited with anticipation. Our mouths watered as we tried to imagine the savory items he would bring back for us. We sipped our stale tea and listened for the sound of footsteps approaching the house.

Finally we heard heavy boots crunching through the snow. I ran to the window, but before I even got there the front door swung open, and Christian and Mr. Anders stood in the doorway! Mr. Anders had a firm grip on Christian's arm, and he glared angrily at Hilde, Hella, and me.

"Tell Mr. Anders how frantic we were when we got separated from the group yesterday," Christian said breathlessly.

I wondered if my face looked as frightened as Hilde's and Hella's.

"Yes, sir, Mr. Anders," I spoke up. "Are we ever glad to see you!"

"That's why we sent Christian out looking for you," Hilde chimed in.

We had lied. Courage to run away did not include courage to face a firing squad.

"The prisoners are all waiting for you at the north end of town," Mr. Anders sneered. "Get your jackets and let's get going. And, Dittman, a word of warning to you. You know I've never liked you. I'm going to be watching you. I don't need much of a reason to kill you; do you know that? What I'm saying is, don't try anything funny like this again. Understand?"

What went wrong? Why hadn't God allowed our escape to be successful? We had tasted freedom for so many hours; now it seemed as though God had granted it to us for a season, but then had changed His mind!

We silently walked back to the formation line, lost in our thoughts and our grief. It had been a dreadful mistake for Christian to leave the safety of the house.

The endless marching resumed in a last effort to outrun the advancing Russians. At least Christian, Hilde, Hella, and I felt refreshed from a good night's sleep. The other prisoners looked as though they were about to drop from the cold and their hunger and exhaustion.

As we marched out of the little village, I spotted an empty child's wagon sitting in a deserted farmyard. Thinking that some of us could pull our bags in it, I foolishly dropped out of the line for a second to retrieve it. Unfortunately Mr. Anders turned around just then and saw me break my marching stride. After his warning of a few moments earlier, I had made a drastic mistake.

Mr. Anders came at me furiously. "Where do you think you're going, you little brat? I told you no more funny stuff!" He pressed a revolver against my heart.

"Sir, I'm sorry. It's just that some of us are weary from marching, and I thought we could pull our bags and knapsacks in this wagon."

"Nonsense!" With that he dragged me several yards until we caught up with the marching prisoners, whose stride had not been broken. After that Mr. Anders would seldom let me out of his sight.

Late that night we arrived at our new camp, which was not far from the abandoned town of Grunberg. The women were placed on the bitterly cold floor. Everyone was too tired to speculate or question.

At five the next morning, we were awakened and ordered to line up in the center of the new camp. From there we were marched for miles down a snow-covered road. Finally we came to an open area where we were assigned the task of hauling rubbish, junk, and bricks from one pile to another. The heavily armed guards stood over us, making sure we moved at a frantic pace. The heavy, monotonous work was exhausting and pointless, simply to keep us occupied for ten hours a day. For some mysterious reason they chose to make us do senseless work rather than shoot us all and bury us in a giant grave. Knowing the Nazi extermination mentality and thirst for blood, we marveled each day that we still had life, especially when we knew that our pitiful rations meant that some soldier on the battlefield had just that much less.

Steffi ran up behind me as we marched back to camp from work one afternoon. Some hidden excitement that I couldn't quite define was in her voice.

"Anita," she said as she tried to whisper her enthusiasm, "take this piece of paper. On it you'll find an address. If I should disappear suddenly, give the address to my mother when you get to Theresienstadt. It's the address of some of our relatives in Bavaria. Tell Mother she can find me there after the war."

"Steffi, what are you talking about? Why are you going to disappear? Where are you going?"

"I can't say. Just deliver the address to Mother. Promise?"

"I promise, but I beg you to tell me what this is all about."

"All I can say is that I might try to escape, but I don't know when or how yet."

"Steffi, be careful! Whatever you do, be careful. I will miss you so much if you go."

Two days later Steffi was mysteriously gone. No one had the slightest idea how she had escaped or if she had made it.

I developed a painful blister on my right heel from the endless marching, walking, hauling, and the rubbing of the wooden shoes. Since we hadn't been able to bathe or wash our clothes in weeks, I feared the blister would become infected and cause real problems.

At the same time I noticed an unusual change in Christian. Without explanation, he became cool toward me. It began ever so slightly, but it soon became obvious that something was wrong. I racked my brain trying to figure out what I had done. Finally I confronted him one evening as we marched home.

He hardly spoke that night. No matter what subject I brought up, he dropped it and became strangely silent. He kept his hands in his pockets so that I couldn't reach out and take his hand; before we had always held hands as we marched from work. I was sure my heart ached far more than my painful blister.

"What have I done, Christian?" I asked sadly as we walked toward the camp.

Christian groped for the right words in the awkward situation.

"I'm sorry," he said. "Someday I can explain, Anita."

And with that inadequate explanation, he marched silently back to camp without even a look my way. I was brokenhearted.

I anguished over the end of our wonderful relationship. It was ten times worse because I didn't know the reason. Had Christian fallen in love with someone else? Was God going to take Christian away from me, too, in an attempt to test my faith? It seemed that I had lost so much that was precious to me in life. Not Christian too! I withdrew into myself because it hurt too badly to talk about it with anyone. But finally, two nights after my talk with Christian, an explanation came.

Christian's sister, Hilde, slept beside me now. As the lights were turned out, I watched as Hilde repacked her knapsack in the dark.

"What are you doing?" I asked curiously. "Can't that wait until morning?"

Hilde remained strangely aloof as she continued to organize her knapsack. It seemed so strange because Hilde and I had grown closer since the incident with Mr. Anders. It was almost as though she was keeping something from me just for my own good.

After work the next day Hilde Risel was missing from camp. Suddenly it all made sense to me. Christian didn't want me to be involved or implicated in his sister's escape plan. He had helped her escape, but he himself did not try to run.

Mr. Anders immediately associated Christian with Hilde's escape plan. The next time I saw Christian, his face was black and blue and full of cuts and bruises. Obviously he had been badly beaten by Anders, yet Anders left me alone, thinking our romance had been severed.

A week later we all awoke to the sound of heavy Russian cannons in the distance. The Russian invasion was nearly at our doorstep! Everyone was on edge that whole day. The guards, particularly, were anxious to receive orders to move on to safety. Siberian prison camps had a reputation for making the German soldier suffer, and few prisoners ever came home from them. All day our guards smoked and paced around us as we worked and listened to the guns of liberation.

The ground shook as the cannon shells burst in the distance. We all worked silently that day, some lost deep in thought and some of us in prayer. How I missed Steffi's close friendship and Christian's strength. The Wolf brothers were gone, and now Hilde. But I still had my little band of believers, and I also had that inner strength and peace that came from Jesus.

It seemed so long since we'd had any definite news of the war. Its turning tide was easily measured by the guards' disposition, but we hungered for specifics. We desperately wanted to know how Russian soldiers behaved as they liberated a town. All we had heard was terrible propaganda, which just might be true. If the Russian soldier was the scoundrel he'd been painted to be, perhaps the distant roar was not the liberating sound we'd been waiting for after all.

Terrible pain had spread to my leg; the blister had become infected. My leg began to discolor; it throbbed so badly that I could barely march back to camp that night after work. I tried to balance on my friend Hella as I limped into camp, still listening to the gunfire in the distance.

"I think this is it!" Hella said hopefully as I clung to her in the food line. "How much closer can they get?"

"They will be here by morning," I said.

As we ate our watery soup, we sat and listened to the ominous sound of war in the distance. My mind went back to my time in Berlin. Somehow, after surviving an air-raid attack, all other threats seemed tame. Little did I realize that I had experienced neither my last—nor my most horrible—air raid. The sounds and smells of war are horrible. And where there is smoke, there are the suffering victims of men's inability to peacefully coexist. I wondered what right I had to sit snugly in my prisoners' compound when others might be dying.

Suddenly the guards rushed us all into our quarters and sealed the doors shut. We were so positioned in our barracks that there was no way to escape if we were directly hit by cannon fire. The women, whose emotions had been pushed to the limit, were frantic as the guards marched around the grounds.

"They all have bayonets on their rifles!" I said to Hella as I looked out the window.

"Do you suppose they're for us?" she asked nervously.

"I don't know. The guards seem to be surrounding our quarters. I can't figure out if they're keeping us in or the Russians out."

We were truly caged animals at the mercy of our keepers—and our liberators. Terror was written all over the women's faces. Some sat motionless on their straw mattresses. This tension was almost too great; most of us had gone through months of torturous labor and deprivation.

All night long the commotion continued as the guns popped in the distance and the guards paced outside our doors and windows. Their shiny bayonets glistened in the moonlight as they marked time waiting for instructions.

Hella Frommelt and Uschi Muller sat alongside me on their straw mattresses. Uschi was one of the married women in the camp; her husband, Helmut, was housed in the men's quarters.

No one slept that night; turmoil reigned inside and outside. Without exception, it was the longest night any of us had known. It seemed almost certain that we could all be under gunfire by morning. At the same time, my leg cried for attention as it continued to swell. I wondered how I could outrun the Russians even if I could escape the Nazi guards with their rifles and bayonets. In the face of such odds, faith could rest nowhere but in God, especially as I thought of Mother and Steffi.

I will lift up mine eyes unto the hills, from whence cometh my help. My help cometh from the LORD, which made heaven and earth.
—Psalms 121:1–2

13

escape

"We should think about making a run for it," Hella said as we sat waiting for the dawn. "The guards are so scared will they care if a few of us are missing?"

"Hella is right," Uschi chimed in. It was true that our ranks had dwindled in recent weeks. Anders and his men had little time to worry about a few runaway prisoners among hundreds. If Christian had not walked right into Anders, we would probably still be free.

"We'll pray for the right opportunity," I said to Uschi and Hella. "When it arises, we'll know it!"

No one moved from her mattress all night as the clock ticked away slowly. The imaginations of all the women—whose emotions had admittedly been stretched to a breaking point—ran away with them.

But toward morning the guards burst into our quarters and gave us just three minutes to gather our few possessions and line up in the center of camp. Confusion grew to pandemonium as the impatient guards shouted their orders. They organized the men in one section of the camp and the women in the other. Every now and then in the early-morning darkness, mortar from a Russian tank lit up the distant sky. The approaching army had two faces, depending on how we wanted to interpret propaganda.

As we shivered in the morning cold, three huge horse carts drove up out of nowhere. The women were ordered to climb in. I saw it as a gift from God; I could never have marched with my leg. But as we women climbed on, we noticed that the men appeared to be staying behind in the camp.

Uschi was frantic as she sat beside me, seeing that she and Helmut would be separated.

"Helmut will be killed!" she cried as Hella and I tried to comfort her. She strained her eyes in the blackness to see Helmut as another twenty-five women piled onto our cart. Our friends Trautel Lindberg and Ursel Engel climbed on and sat next to us.

"Trust God for him, Uschi," I pleaded with her as the guards hurried us. "He is the only hope any of us have. Helmut will be all right."

"It is easy for you to say, Anita!"

"Uschi, I trust my mother to Jesus every day!" I insisted.

The drivers of our horse carts were Polish prisoners of war who had served as slave laborers for the nearby German farmers. Our driver was a young Pole with hair almost as dark as the night. At the command of a guard, he gave the horse a slap, and we quickly headed out of camp toward the cobblestone road. I listened to the pitiful cries of the married women who were being separated from their husbands. The men prisoners grew smaller in the distance as our horse cart bounced over deep ruts in the road. As we rode away, I strained for a glimpse of Gunther or Christian, but all the men's faces had become indistinct.

Behind our three horse carts, each loaded with dozens of frightened women, were only two guards—on bicycles! They presented an absurdly comic scene as they tried to pedal their bikes in the snow and keep up with the carts. They rode and fell, rode and fell, before they found their balance.

"This whole situation is just made for an escape," I whispered to

Uschi, Hella, Trautel, and Ursel. "Those two guards can't possibly keep track of all of us."

"And Anders isn't with us," Hella exclaimed. "He stayed with the men."

"When should we do it?" Uschi asked, the tears still glistening on her cheeks.

"Not now," I answered as the others looked to me for direction. "God must show us the perfect time. We can't do it a minute before that."

"But how will we know when that is?" Hella asked.

"I'll know, Hella," I said.

Most of the women on the horse carts stared blankly into the air. Cold and frightened, many had forgotten how to hope. And those who had been with their husbands were struggling with their sudden separation.

"Uschi, do you still have those cigarettes?" I asked with a scheme in mind.

Uschi nodded.

"Somehow I want to bribe our Polish driver," I said softly. "Do you have any money? Just a small amount?"

Uschi had been well-to-do before her internment, but it was Hella who pulled out a bill of twenty marks and showed it to us.

"Good," I said. "When the time is right, let me do the talking."

"Anita, it will never work!" Hella insisted. "Cigarettes and money aren't enough. We will be shot if he's caught."

After we had traveled several hours, the gunfire grew faint in the distance. Along our journey we passed a small train station, and a few miles later we arrived at our new home. Treacherous-looking barbed-wire fences circled the camp, with huge, ugly barracks in the center. It almost appeared to be a deserted death camp. All of us were amazed that so many of these camps dotted the German countryside. Hardly anyone in Germany could know the extent of the Nazis' extermination system.

The huge entrance gate swung open, and two of the horse carts moved inside the camp. Ours remained outside for a moment as the two guards chatted together.

"Your plan is crazy!" Ursel said to me. "Trautel, Uschi, and I are going to make a run for it through the woods. You and Hella come with us."

"I can't. My leg will never carry me."

"I'm staying with Anita," Hella insisted.

As the two guards continued to confer inside the gate, Trautel, Uschi, and Ursel jumped down from the cart and dashed into the nearby woods. The other women looked on silently, too numb and frightened to react, and certainly not daring enough to join them. As we watched them leap through mounds of snow, we held our breath, hoping the guards would not see them. In less than a minute they had disappeared into the thick cover of the woods. Hella and I looked at each other and breathed a noticeable sigh of relief as the woods swallowed them up.

Finally the two guards separated and one came our way. "What should we do now?" Hella whispered desperately.

"It's now or never!"

"I need two of you to go and pick up some things for the camp," the guard commanded.

I spoke up instantly. "Hella and I will go, sir."

"The rest of you get down, then. Into the camp immediately! Driver, take these two to the factory down the street and make sure they get these supplies." He handed our Polish driver a list of items. "I will join you in just a moment."

Our hearts raced with excitement as we saw God set up the perfect escape. Now if we could only bribe the Polish driver!

"Hurry up, now!" the guard commanded one last time.

When the last woman got off the cart, the driver headed down the country road toward a small factory. Hella and I moved up nearer to him.

"To the train station," I begged as I flashed the cigarettes and the money in front of his eyes. "We beg you; take us there immediately!"

Only God could carry out this impossible plan. What was in it for the driver except a little money, the cigarettes, and probably severe punishment? But an amused smile came over his face, and he slapped the horse with a makeshift whip. Hella and I nearly fell to the floor of the cart as the horse lunged full speed ahead. The driver slipped the cigarettes and the money into his pocket without saying a word. A look of delight was on his face. Maybe he was too dumb to realize what he was doing. Then again, maybe God had given us an angel as our driver!

"Do you remember where the railroad station is?" I asked him.

He nodded his head. Hella and I clung to the horse cart as we bounced frantically along. The camp grew small in the distance until it was out of sight.

"This time we will make it, Hella!" I said confidently. "God would not give us the perfect escape opportunity only to let us get caught again."

The warmth of the midmorning sun could hardly penetrate the cold air and wind that blew in our faces. But it didn't matter; the prospect of our freedom stirred up a warmth of its own within us.

Since the railroad station was only minutes from the camp, it came into view quickly. From the horse cart we saw about a dozen villagers roaming about the area and several more inside the station.

In the train yard stood a long freight train consisting almost entirely of flatcars. On each flatcar sat an army tank. Several German soldiers seemed to be inspecting the train as they walked alongside it balancing their giant rifles.

"Stop here," I begged the driver again as we came within several yards of the train and the station. Hella and I climbed down from the cart, and my leg burned with pain as I accidentally landed on it. It was as though God was reminding me that He had allowed us to flee to the railroad station by horse cart rather than on foot just so I wouldn't have to hike on my swollen leg.

The Polish driver quickly turned the cart around and left. How incredible it was that God had sent us such a driver to carry us one step further in our attempt at freedom! He had asked for so little, and he surely risked his life. His eyes had sparkled as he caught a glimpse of the excitement on our faces. As he headed down the road leading away from the train station, he turned and waved good-bye. Hella and I wondered what kind of fate lay ahead for this angel in disguise.

While we stood at a distance, watching the activity at the train station, we heard footsteps coming up behind us. Hella and I turned around and saw Uschi, Ursel, and Trautel come out of the woods and head for us! God had timed their arrival at the train station perfectly. Surely He was at the very center of this whole escape plan.

Uschi, Ursel, and Trautel listened in disbelief as Hella and I told them about our horse-cart driver.

"We must look like fleeing villagers now," I said to the others. "I'm going to ask one of those soldiers if we can ride the freight train out of here. It is too dangerous to wait for another train. You let me do the talking."

"Anita, they will never let us ride on that train!" Hella said.

"It's worth a try. Trust me."

As we casually walked toward the train station, we tried to control any unusual fear that might be on our faces. Certainly, we were allowed some fear, since the Russian artillery could be heard again in the distance. But extreme panic might give us away.

I walked directly toward a handsome soldier who stood alongside a flatcar loaded with a demolished tank. He gave me a broad smile as he saw me approach.

"My friends and I are dreadfully afraid of the Russians," I said to the soldier. "Would you allow us to ride your train out of here?"

"You want to ride inside a demolished Russian tank, kid?" he asked. "It would be a long, cold ride to our next stop."

"It's all right with us, sir. We would rather do that than be captured by the Reds."

The soldier seemed amused at the prospect of sharing a tank ride with five girls.

"Let me check with my commanding officer, then," he replied as he walked toward the train station. "If he agrees, it's all right with me."

The soldier walked inside the station while the girls stood a few yards away, nervously surveying the situation. Moments later he returned, a broad grin on his face.

"He says you can ride with me," the soldier announced. "My name is Waldemar Stricker. What is your name?"

"I am Anita, and those are my good friends." I turned and waved at the girls to come over. "They are Uschi, Hella, Ursel, and Trautel. Our families fled the village here a week ago, and we're hoping to join them in Sorau."

Fear of the invading Russian army had inspired this fabrication. In less than three months I would know how well-founded these fears were. But God was already preparing my deliverance—beginning with the blister on my heel.

"Well, climb in this tank, then. I'll help you up. We go right through Sorau."

I nearly forgot about the constant pain in my leg as our freedom drew closer and closer. Waldemar lifted the five of us onto the tank and then lowered us down into its crowded compartment. We sat close together so that we could all fit into the space designed for about three people. Then Waldemar dropped down inside the tank and squeezed into the center of the five of us. We all wanted to burst into laughter over the absurdity of the moment and over the tension of the escape plan. Moments later a whistle blew and the train inched forward. The five of us tried to fight back any tears that might give us away.

"Would you like some sandwiches?" Waldemar asked.

Our eyes lit up! "Oh, Waldemar, God bless you!" I exclaimed.

"Are you a believer?" he asked me as he reached into a bag for some food.

"Yes!"

"So am I!" he exclaimed.

Oh, how good God is! Could He have sent us another angel in disguise? I wanted to hit Waldemar with a round of questions: How could he support a cause that exterminated Jews if he was a believer? How could he serve the devil Hitler? How could he kill innocent people by supporting the cause of this awful war?

As we slowly glided along the countryside, another soldier opened the tank's hatch door and lowered himself down.

"I brought some hot tea," he announced with a smile, obviously amused at the idea of girls riding in the tank.

Introduced as Klaus, he managed to find just enough room so that we all could fit in snugly. No suspicion was in the soldiers' eyes as we laughed about our predicament. Rather, they were gracious and kind, and appreciative of having company for the lengthy ride to Sorau.

"Say, my little friend," Waldemar said to me, "you are shivering. Let me help you keep warm." Waldemar shed part of his outer uniform and wrapped me up in it, and then he put his strong arm around me to add further warmth. Taking his cue from Waldemar, Klaus followed suit and did the same for Hella.

I wanted to talk about the war, but it was too risky. Waldemar and Klaus would have the inside story, I was sure. Klaus was not a believer and seemed nervous whenever I mentioned God's protection over me. So instead we asked all about the two soldiers and learned that they were among the few lucky ones to return from the Russian battlefront. They told of the tragedy of the war there, how thousands of German soldiers had frozen to death on their way to Moscow.

The German war strategists had planned on a swift victory during the summer months of 1941. Instead they ran head-on into a stubborn Red army that caused the battle to be dragged on into the winter. German men and machines froze that winter while the Russian army was prepared for the winter onslaught. It had been a drastic and fatal miscalculation on the part of the Germans, just as my mother had thought.

Our tank had dozens of shell holes in the top; as the snow began to fall, the large flakes landed on us. Nevertheless, exhaustion overtook us, and we leaned on the soldiers' broad shoulders and fell asleep. However, we had instructed them to awaken us at Sorau.

Sometime later the jerking of the train awakened me. Looking out the shell holes, I could see it was pitch dark.

"Where are we?" I asked sleepily.

"About forty miles from Berlin," Waldemar replied. I realized Sorau had come and gone and we hadn't stopped.

"Why didn't you let us off at Sorau?" I asked, sounding very irritated.

"My dear little friend," Waldemar said as he tightened his arm around me, "I just wanted to protect you. My little radio here informed us that the Russians were about to launch a major attack on Sorau. We sped rapidly through the town. There was no time to stop, and you certainly could not have jumped from a moving train."

Tears welled up in my eyes as I thought of Father. He loved to remind me how peaceful Sorau was—so peaceful he didn't need God. I wondered if the present circumstances would make him cry out for God's mercy.

"We are going to get out here for a short break," Waldemar

announced. "We are at a little train station where we can use the washroom and get a few rations."

The pain in my leg had intensified, and I didn't know how I would ever climb out of the clumsy Russian tank. But Waldemar and Klaus gently lifted all of us out of the hatch.

"I'm not sure I can walk on my leg," I said to the soldiers as I rolled up my pant leg. My leg was twice its normal size.

"What happened?" Waldemar asked.

"It started out as a blister and got infected from dirt. It has been getting worse for some time."

"You must get help for it," Waldemar said as he leaned down to examine the ugly blue color of my leg. "You will lose the leg if you don't get some help."

Waldemar lifted me up and carried me to the ladies' room. Then he gave me a clean toothbrush, some toothpaste, a bar of soap, and a clean towel. What luxuries! Klaus gave Hella similar items. After we'd been delivered to the ladies' room, we stood inside and giggled over the absurdity of our situation.

"I think they're guardian angels!" I told the others. "God has sent them to carry us to freedom; I just know it."

"Anita, what should we do?" Hella asked. "We can't go into Berlin! It's just a shell of a city, and it's too dangerous. We don't want to go into any city that is being hit from the air."

"I know," I said.

"We can try to find my relatives in Bautzen," Uschi suggested. "Do you think it is safe there?" I asked.

"Bautzen is a small town. Surely the Allies wouldn't try to overtake it or bomb it," Uschi answered. "Maybe we could spend the rest of the war there with my relatives."

"Are they Jews?" Hella asked.

"No," she answered.

"Good! Then perhaps they are alive and well," I said enthusiastically. "I vote for Bautzen."

"I think Ursel and I will try for Rostock," Trautel said. "I have friends there who will hide us."

"There is safety in numbers," Hella said. "You should stay with us."

"No, I have made up my mind," Trautel replied. "I must go to Rostock."

When we came out of the bathroom, Waldemar and Klaus were waiting with what looked to be starvation rations for a soldier. They'd gotten only some hot tea, rolls with butter, and two eggs. Even so, they graciously shared everything with us. Waldemar insisted that I eat one of the eggs to give me strength. While we ate, he put his protective arm around me again.

"Waldemar ," I said sadly, "since we could not get out at Sorau and find our families, we have decided to go to Bautzen and Rostock. Can you help us get there?"

A pensive look came over both the soldiers' faces. Our company had obviously been a high spot in their army career.

"I am sad to see you go, little one," Waldemar replied. "I had hoped our friendship would be a long one."

"But we must find our families, Waldemar," I said. "You understand that, don't you? We have no one in Berlin. Trautel has friends in Rostock, and Uschi has relatives in Bautzen."

"Rostock is just a shell, I'm afraid," Waldemar said. "The Allies have hit it from the air."

"We'll go there anyway," Trautel replied.

"Well, all right then," Waldemar agreed. "Our next stop is Furstenwalde, a suburb of Berlin. The two of you can catch a train directly to Rostock. Anita, you and the others will have to take a train from Furstenwalde to Dresden and then change trains for Bautzen. Plan on a long wait at each station. Trains don't run on time, you know. The Allies have hit a lot of our railroads. Come now; we must get back into our sardine can."

Waldemar and Klaus lifted us back into the tank and we rode quietly for another twenty miles. Waldemar scribbled an address on a piece of paper and handed it to me as we journeyed the last few miles with the soldiers.

"Here is my address, Anita," he said. "You will write me, won't you? Only God knows when our paths will cross again. I pray it will be soon."

"I will write," I promised, "and I will pray for you every day."

Waldemar leaned over and gave me a kiss on the cheek.

A few moments later the freight train rolled to a stop at Furstenwalde, and Waldemar and Klaus lifted us out again.

"They were wonderful!" Hella exclaimed about Klaus and Waldemar as the train sped out of sight. "I think Anita is right when she talks about angels."

Although I had purposed to use Mother's money for her freedom, the opportunity had never presented itself. So I bought freedom for Uschi and Hella and me—tickets to Dresden and then to Bautzen. I might even have a little left over for an emergency. Surely God was meeting all of our needs.

Ursel and Trautel had scraped up barely enough money from their camp wages to buy tickets to Rostock. But it was another miracle because the guards had usually found a reason to keep our pitiful monthly wages themselves. The money Mother had left me was a special gift from God since Hella, Uschi, and I had never been given any of our supposed wages.

It was midmorning when the train for Rostock arrived, and we bade Ursel and Trautel goodbye. Uschi, Hella, and I had to wait nearly six hours for a train to Dresden, and it was nearly dark outside by the time we boarded. I leaned back in the dirty, overcrowded train and tried to bask in my newfound freedom.

Thoughts drifted to so many loved ones: Mother, Father, Steffi, Christian, Rudi, Gerhard, Wolfgang, Joachim, the Rosens, Ann, Gunther, and my three aunts. Separation was one of the worst parts of a war, and the uncertainty about the safety of a loved one made it even more difficult. If Berlin hadn't been such a burned-out shell of a city, and if I had had relatives there, I would have liked to go and look up Ruth Conrad and her family, who so graciously had given me food during my stay with Mrs. Michaelis. But it seemed right to go to Bautzen, which just maybe the war had avoided. Also, I knew that my throbbing leg desperately needed medical attention.

Sometime after midnight we arrived at a train station in a suburb of Dresden called Arnsbach. It was Monday, February 12, 1945. For a while we sat sleepily in the train station, waiting for our connection to Bautzen. Suddenly the air-raid sirens began to wail, and panicking people began to scurry toward the shelter beneath the station. Hella and Uschi headed there, too, but I knew my leg could not carry me down the endless flight of stairs. Hella and Uschi looked at me in horror as they realized that I was staying behind.

"I can't make it!" I told them. "You go without me. Go, I beg you. Don't worry about me!"

Their faces were contorted with fear and worry over me; but as we heard the first bomb scream through the air, they turned and dashed toward the shelter.

I ran into the street, thinking it might be safer if I wasn't inside a building. All too often people were entombed in buildings when the walls fell in. As I looked up, I saw dozens of bombers streaming across the sky, and then I heard the sickening sound of whistling bombs falling through the air. Finally they hit their targets, and the earth around me went into convulsions.

"Dear God," I pleaded, "I can pass through this safely only with Your help."

Suddenly giant flames appeared everywhere, and Dresden turned into a bright orange glow. And like thunder after lightning came the deafening reports of the bombs. Monstrous fireworks buried uncounted thousands of Germans. I was in the middle of Dresden's famous firestorm, produced by the rush of air from the intense heat. Huge columns of smoke blanked out the stars and moon.

From out of nowhere streamed hundreds of dazed residents. Many had mutilated bodies and wept with pain and grief. Terrified children roamed the area, looking for their parents.

I buried my head in my hands and wept for Germany and her tortured people. How could I live with this memory the rest of my life? How I longed to scoop all of Dresden's suffering humanity into my arms and tell them about Jesus' saving power. For so many it was too late, but some were now before the mouth of hell, and I felt sure they would listen.

After what seemed like only moments, the bombs stopped falling. An eerie hush fell over the burning city. It was the hush of death, broken only by the faint cries of her trapped and dying. More than 135,000 perished in the raid.

The train station had escaped a direct hit, and its frightened occupants scurried to the surface when the all-clear siren wailed. When Hella and Uschi surveyed the destruction all around us, they couldn't believe that we had survived. Neither could they believe that I had stood unharmed in the center of the street as buildings fell all around me.

"I have a great big God," I told them. "For some reason He wants me alive. It is the only explanation."

Ambulance sirens wailed for hours that night as Germany tried to bandage her wounded and dying. Since the train station was one of dozens of makeshift hospitals, we watched the wounded being carried in. Hundreds of victims were attended to by a handful of doctors and nurses who had survived the firestorm.

The suffering of the innocent because of man's inability to keep peace on earth will always be engraved on my mind.

Nuremberg, Germany 1945. *Courtesy United States Holocaust Memorial Museum*

14

HOSPITALIZED

Bautzen was a clean little town that had escaped the war's destruction. Uschi's relatives pampered us when we found them, and they took me to the local hospital almost immediately. I could see that the hospital was run by Nazis, and something about them told me they still hadn't given up the "glorious" dream of the Third Reich.

The head nurse, Miss Grete, had to cut away my sock, which clung to my swollen leg. The infection had driven my temperature up to nearly 105 degrees.

While she worked on my leg, Miss Grete looked at me, the ugly Nazi pin on her uniform transfixing my gaze. Obviously she didn't appreciate the fact that I didn't respond to her "Heil Hitler" when we met. She gave me a skimpy hospital gown and walked with me to a room at the end of the hall. I climbed between the clean, white sheets, almost delirious from fever. However, it seemed that I was placed at the bottom of the staff's priority list; I lay for hours waiting for treatment. Finally I lost all track of time as I drifted in and out of consciousness. Often I heard footsteps in the hall, but they never came into my room.

Two days later emergency surgery was performed: two holes were drilled into my foot to enable the infection to drain. Since ether was at a high premium, I wasn't given enough, and I awakened in the middle of the surgery. Amid the pain, I heard Miss Grete say, "She sure talked, didn't she, Doctor?"

I was numb with fear, sensing that I'd given myself away. My fear was confirmed in the following days and weeks as the Nazi hospital staff neglected me in various subtle ways. Besides being left unattended for hours, I was never given any pain pills. Because I always refused to respond to Miss Grete's "Heil Hitler," she withheld the necessary sanitary bandages for my leg wound. She also rerouted the doctor's visits so that I would often be missed for a day or two. Due to that kind of treatment and because I developed an allergy to the medication, I had to endure six long weeks of loneliness and neglect in the hospital. Only frequent visits from Hella made it bearable.

My leg was cut and sewed hastily and improperly in four operations. Six ugly red scars would be the result. Just prior to the last operation, a Nazi doctor said, "Anita, we must insert some more drainage tubes in your leg. This is serious because we will be working so close to an artery. If it gets complicated, we may have to amputate your leg."

How I needed Mother's comforting words of assurance during those hours before my operation! What was to stop these Nazis from cutting off my leg because of their dislike for me? I could only talk to my heavenly Father, as once again I relied totally upon Him. He faithfully demonstrated His love for me, for I learned Miss Grete's day off that week was the day of my surgery. At least she wouldn't be in the operating room, encouraging an amputation.

Again I was given only enough ether to put me into a light sleep, so I heard the voices of the doctors and nurses throughout most of the surgery. The pain was so intense that I hoped I would just black out.

After the operation, as I lay there gritting my teeth, I felt beneath the cover for my leg. Praise God, it was still there! I believed

God would surely spare it because He knew I had a long journey to Theresienstadt.

I felt it again as I was wheeled back to my dingy little room. Tears trickled out of the corners of my eyes as I realized that God's mercy had kept me in one piece.

Hella visited me that night and, as usual, kept me up to date on the war.

"The Allied troops are in nearly every major city now, Anita, and they're on the outskirts of Berlin. The war will be finished in a few days, but the bad news is that the Russians are advancing on Bautzen too. They may be here any day."

We had hoped and prayed that the war would end without an invasion of Bautzen, for we continued to be afraid of the Russians, not knowing how they would treat us. Would they pillage, burn, and rape, or would they liberate and restore? We had been fed horrible propaganda about the Reds. According to Hitler, they were as despicable as the Jews. How would the Russians know that Hella, Uschi, and I were victims of the war and not perpetrators? These questions jumbled my thoughts as I lay recuperating.

Hella also told me that President Roosevelt had died that week. I felt so bad that the man who had stepped in and speeded up my freedom hadn't lived to see our victory celebration.

When I pulled back the covers to show Hella my ugly leg wounds, which would leave lifelong scars, she gasped.

"Don't worry, Hella," I said calmly. "Those wounds and scars will be my salvation. God has impressed that on me as I've been lying here all these weeks. He says all things work together for our good, and so will these wounds."

That week Hella came to the hospital every day and helped me learn to walk again. I worked frantically to get back the strength in my leg so I could make the long journey into Czechoslovakia to find Mother.

More than six weeks after I'd been admitted to the hospital, I was told I could leave. That morning I awakened with renewed enthusiasm for life; the ordeal was over. But before I could even begin to collect myself or my things, I heard Miss Grete's frantic voice in the hall.

"Out of bed, all who are able!" she screamed. "Get dressed immediately and go to the air-raid shelter. The Russians are in Bautzen! Hurry up!"

I struggled to get dressed as the frightened hospital staff and patients scurried about, but I was still weak and had very little strength in my leg. Even so, that unexplainable peace from God overcame me again.

As I reached for the cane I'd been given, I heard gunfire in the streets. Intermittently I also heard the sound of cannon fire; we all knew that one blast from a Russian cannon could level a building.

Slowly I moved down the hall, leaning on the wall and balancing on my cane. When Miss Grete saw me with the cane, she yanked it from me; I nearly crashed to the floor.

"That old lady over there needs this!" she insisted. "Go and help her into the shelter."

"Oh, dear God, give me double strength," I pleaded softly. Only God could strengthen and steady me as I balanced both the elderly patient and myself going down the shelter stairs.

Nearly a hundred patients and staff walked, ran, or were pushed in wheelchairs to the air-raid shelter deep beneath the hospital. Again I heard the pitiful cries of desperate people whose ailing bodies protested the move to the cold, damp shelter.

God had pity on us, for just as the air-raid shelter door closed, we heard a blast of mortar tear through the hospital's first floor. We thought that surely it was an accident, that the Russians wouldn't knowingly shell a hospital caring for civilians. But then another round of mortar hit the hospital. All day long gunfire sounded in the streets as German soldiers tried to save the city, but there was no stopping the Allies anymore.

I was so afraid for Hella and Uschi and her relatives. But I could only leave them in God's hands, as it seemed I had to do so often with loved ones.

For eight days we huddled in the candlelit shelter while the Germans tried in vain to save the town. Four of us patients shared one tiny bed. We could hardly move; otherwise, we would push someone on the floor. Some patients cursed while others wept or pleaded for help, but the hospital staff had been able to carry in only a few medical supplies. We had little food, and it seemed that the shelter was pitifully prepared for a long ordeal. Evidently no one had wanted to admit that a day might come when so many would be crammed into the shelter.

I tried to comfort the three elderly women who shared my bed.

"Do you know Jesus?" I asked them one by one. "Because He has promised us eternal life after death, we needn't be so afraid. He says that even if we walk through the valley of the shadow of death, we need fear nothing, for He is with us."

They listened as I comforted them and quoted a few Bible passages I had memorized. I had lost my Bible in the confusion of our prison escape. I reached into my pocket to feel my only possessions: a toothbrush, a small bar of soap, a broken comb, and the last of the money Mother had given me.

"Hitler became my god," one of the women admitted. "We thought he was the savior of the country. He promised us so much ..."

"It was only in the last few months that I realized he was a demagogue," another confessed. "Such a dream. Such a nightmare. Can God ever forgive us?"

"Yes, He can!" I replied enthusiastically. "That is what He specializes in. He could forgive even Hitler if he asked for forgiveness. That's how gracious God is."

"I believed in God once," an old lady said, "but it is difficult to believe in Him now. I've seen such ugliness. I lived in Berlin but fled to Bautzen to be with my daughter. Berlin is just a shell, you know. Most of my friends died."

"And what about your daughter?" I asked. "Is she all right?"

"How can I know when I'm trapped down here? I hear the cannon fire and the gunfire outside. How do I know it isn't meant for my daughter and her family?"

"The gunfire has to be for the German soldiers and not innocent civilians," I said, trying to comfort the old lady. "I am going to pray for your daughter now. Would you like to pray with me?"

"Yes, I would," she said.

* * *

About the fourth day of the battle, it grew very quiet outside. Obviously the battle had gone one way or another, and we soon received our answer as a dozen or more Russian soldiers stormed into the air-raid shelter. Everyone stood or sat frozen with fear as the Russians surveyed our pitiful lot. Carrying huge rifles with bayonets on them, they talked among themselves and began to eye the women staff and patients. Then, one by one, they grabbed some of the women and threw them to the floor. While the rest of us looked on in horror, they raped a dozen or more women.

Two of the huge soldiers came right for me. "Oh, God, help me," I pleaded out loud. Pulling me from the bed, they threw me to the floor and started to rip off my clothes. It was a scene right out of hell, as man's depraved nature was personified before my eyes.

The two soldiers gazed at my unbandaged leg, with its horrible red wounds that were only partially healed. They grimaced as they saw the leg and muttered to each other. Then they shook their heads and walked away from me in search of a more appealing victim. So this was the salvation promised by my wounds!

When the horror ended an hour later, we all sat in a state of semi-shock, wondering what to do and where to go. Found, conquered, abandoned. Was that it? Despair wore many faces that day: fear, confusion, agony, loneliness. Were all Germans suffering like this as they came under the guns of the Allies?

I saw a woman weeping as she sat on the floor in a corner. In the darkness of the shelter I couldn't make out who it was. I limped over to see if I could help, or at least listen to her problem. It was Miss Grete. I prayed that God might give me humility and compassion to reach out and comfort her.

I timidly knelt beside her and put my arm around her shoulder. She didn't pull away, even though she knew who I was. Instead, she leaned her head against my shoulder and wept. In broken sentences she told me that she had been raped four times by the Russian soldiers.

"God have mercy on them," I said.

She looked up at me with red, swollen eyes. "How can you comfort me?" she asked. "I really wanted to kill you after you talked on the operating table and we found out that you are Jewish."

"Jesus tells us to love our enemies and to do good to those who persecute us," I answered. "He loved even those who drove Him to the cross, and He begged His Father's forgiveness for them."

Miss Grete's grief was not just from the physical assault she had suffered; it came from the broken vision of the glorious Fatherland—the realization that Hitler, the pied piper she had followed, was a fraud. The Third Reich had finally caused her pain—in its fall.

"Ye have heard that it hath been said, Thou shalt love thy neighbour, and hate thine enemy. But I say unto you, Love your enemies, bless them that curse you, do good to them that hate you, and pray for them which despitefully use you, and persecute you."
—Matthew 5:43–44

15

eND of a jouRNey

"Go home now, Anita," the German doctor said to me. "There is nothing more we can do for your leg. It is healing well."

Where is home? I thought. Bautzen lay in ruins, and I could not locate Hella or Uschi and her family. I had heard that Sorau was devastated. Somehow I would walk or hitchhike or take a train to Theresienstadt and try to find Mother.

The Führer had put a revolver to his head the day before, while the Russians were on the steps of the parliament building in Berlin, raising the Red flag. Just as Pastor Hornig had predicted, Hitler never gave up until the enemy was at his doorstep.

The Führer was dead, and Germany was in ruins, but at last the war was over. The Reich's twelve-year reign fell far short of its thousand-year dream. Few of its goals were accomplished. It wasn't just Germany that had to try to bounce back now; indeed, the whole world was struggling to get back on its feet.

I dragged my aching leg to the nearby railroad station in Bautzen, grieving at the destruction I saw along the way. I realized that it was multiplied many times over in Germany and throughout Europe.

Miraculously, I had just enough money to get inside Czechoslovakia and also to purchase a passport, but the steps involved in getting there were long and painstaking. Total confusion greeted me wherever I went, for Germany was a leaderless country. No one ever seemed to know who was in charge. Long layovers occurred in city after city en route to Theresienstadt. I was directed to refugee camps where I often spent half a day waiting in line for food rations. But another gnawing never left: Had Mother survived Theresienstadt?

In the town of Asch, near the Czech border, I was directed to an office to obtain a passport. A kind old man with thick glasses assisted me as I filled out the necessary forms to gain entrance into Czechoslovakia. As he learned that I had lost my family and had spent time at Camp Barthold, he sympathetically made sure I filled everything out correctly. In his eyes there seemed to be some unspoken hesitation, which he finally verbalized.

"Why do you want to go into Czechoslovakia, young lady?"

"My mother is in Theresienstadt," I replied. "I must find her."

"Do you know anything about Theresienstadt?" he asked.

"No. No one seems to know much about it."

"The Russians liberated it a while back, of course. They got the terrible typhoid epidemic under control, too. As a matter of fact, the Russians liberated the camp just one day before all the prisoners were to be gassed. Gas chambers were frantically being built by the prisoners themselves. The Germans were forcing them to do it, hoping to exterminate them before the Russians arrived, but the prisoners stalled and stalled while they built the chambers. I don't want to discourage you, young lady, but many of the prisoners there have died."

"I have fought for life only to be reunited with my mother," I answered.

"Then you really shouldn't go into Czechoslovakia alone. The Czechs don't act kindly toward anyone who speaks German. I suggest that you pretend you are a deaf-mute, and don't speak to anyone unless you absolutely have to."

"I appreciate your kind words of warning," I said as he stamped and stapled my papers. "I will do as you say, and I pray that I can accept whatever awaits me at Theresienstadt. I think God will reward me for my faith."

Moments later, he handed me my passport.

"You must go from here to Prague and then change trains to Leitmeritz. From Leitmeritz it is about eight kilometers to Theresienstadt. You may have to walk or hitchhike that distance. Do you have any money at all?"

"No, sir. I've given you my last bit of money for the passport."

"I'm sorry that I cannot help you."

After spending the afternoon in line for rations, I boarded the train from Asch to Prague. It was a beautiful early summer evening, and the countryside was peaceful at last. I was on the final leg of a journey that had begun eighteen months earlier with Mother's arrest.

As it grew dark, we crossed the border into Czechoslovakia, where dozens of Czechs boarded the train. Remembering the old man's words, I kept to myself and stared blankly out the window. The young Czechs laughed as they roamed up and down the aisle, and suddenly I felt trapped in a moving tomb if they should want to harm me. As I looked out into the darkness, I felt a hand on my shoulder. Startled, I turned to look into the face of a handsome young man with dark, curly hair. He sat down next to me and began speaking a strange language. I was trapped.

"I don't understand," I replied.

"*Amerikanski?*" he asked.

I reached into my pocket and pulled out my passport that had all the details on it, including my Jewish background. As he studied the passport, his bright eyes lit up and then filled with tears.

"Shalom, my friend!" he exclaimed in broken German. "I am a Jew, too, returning from a concentration camp. My home is Prague. Where are you going?"

"Theresienstadt, to see if my mother is there."

"I will take you there, my friend, and see that you get on the right train. It is too dangerous for a pretty young lady like you to be traveling alone."

"Oh, you are an angel from heaven!" I said. "God has sent me several like you." Tears rolled down both our faces as we embraced, the language of universal love and understanding. Because of our mutual suffering, we were instantly united.

Peter had been worked nearly to death in a work camp. Most of his comrades didn't survive the ordeal, and many had starved to death. Peter's young and handsome face was gaunt and tired.

I told him that I was a believer in Jesus, but it made no difference to him, though he was a fairly religious Jew. His family had been killed in the war, and he was heading home to Prague to get official news of his loved ones. Going back to the Jewish ghetto in Prague or to Camp Theresienstadt would be like walking into a burned-out building to see if someone were still alive.

At Prague we changed trains for Leitmeritz, and there Peter found a young policeman who would escort me the remaining eight kilometers to Theresienstadt. Peter gave me 150 crowns to use as spending money in Czechoslovakia. Although equivalent to only a few dollars, it provided a feeling of adequacy.

I turned to the Czechoslovakian policeman who planned to drive me the eight kilometers in his jeep. I explained my situation to him and told him about Mother. His beautiful brown eyes looked worried as I shared my overwhelming enthusiasm for the last leg of my journey. It was the same look of concern that the old man had given me, and it said, in so many words, *Child, don't get your hopes up.*

I turned to bid Peter farewell, but he was gone!

"Do you believe in angels?" I asked the policeman as I squinted into the darkness.

"I don't know," he replied.

"I do," I said softly. "I believe I've just met another one. It's Peter. You know, I don't even know his last name."

"Young lady, you pray that the same God who sends you angels has kept your mother alive. Those who didn't die from starvation or overwork were killed off in the epidemic. Let's go now."

We bumped along the unpaved road for about twenty minutes. I tried to blank out the chatter of the friendly Czech policeman, so graciously driving me to Theresienstadt. I really needed to be alone with my thoughts.

As we drove along, it began to get faintly light; I estimated it to be about 6:00 a.m. I was utterly exhausted from weeks of travel. In the predawn light I could make out Theresienstadt in the distance. It had grown from a camp to a city, a city surrounded by huge brick walls. The handful of survivors had remained in Theresienstadt after the war—they had no place to go. Like so many impounded dogs, they waited for relatives to come and claim them.

As we drove closer to the entrance gate, my heart sank. I could make out a giant skull and crossbones painted on it, along with a sign that read: Absolutely No Entrance. Two Russian guards looked as though they wouldn't have much pity for me.

"Please, sir," I said to one of them, "I've traveled for weeks to get here and find my mother. I beg you to let me in."

"Our orders are to let no one in," he answered. "Can't you see the sign? This place is quarantined. There's been a terrible epidemic here."

"I don't care, sir; I'll take that chance. I must see if Hilde Dittman is alive."

"I have my orders, kid."

Suddenly the many long years of disappointment and heartache surfaced and burst; I heaved with sobs. Burying my head in my hands, I let years of sadness spill out in tears.

"The epidemic is over, I've been told," my policeman friend said to the guards. "Why not let her in? She has come a long way."

The two guards conferred with one another while I continued to weep like a small child. If God could ever touch anyone with an ounce of mercy, I prayed He would do so to these men who blocked my entrance into Theresienstadt.

"All right then," one of them said as he reached for the gate handle. "Drive her to the main office, that white building down the street. Then turn around and get out of here."

"Oh, thank you, sir!" I exclaimed, my face wet with tears.

My gracious policeman-turned-chauffeur drove through the gate and dropped me off in front of the main building. On the rickety steps of the main office building, I watched him speed back out the gate. The camp area was strangely deserted. But the morning was still early. From the top of the stairs, I surveyed the sprawling city; it stretched for blocks in several directions. I listened to the eerie silence, broken only by the rustling of a Russian flag waving in the wind near the entrance.

I turned and entered the office area just as an elderly, gray-haired lady was reporting to work.

"Excuse me, ma'am," I said to her as she straightened her desk to begin the workday. "Is this where I might inquire about a certain prisoner? I am Anita Dittman, and I am looking for my mother, Hilde."

"The name is not familiar," she replied. "Let me check." Going to a folder, she thumbed through hundreds of names.

As her fingers came toward the end of the list, she frowned. "She's not listed," she said, "but there is one more place I should check. Wait here."

She walked into another file room and was gone for nearly ten minutes. The waiting was the worst agony I had yet known! My head throbbed from fatigue and hunger—and the tension of the moment. Despite the relatively cool June morning, I broke into perspiration.

Oh, dear God, give me strength to hear her answer, I prayed silently. *I can't believe I've been brought this far only to be disappointed!*

The old lady came out of the file room wearing a broad smile.

"Hilde Dittman is alive and well," she announced. "She is living here in the camp, along with several other women, at this address. I believe she is on the third floor. It's an old building at the very end of this street."

"Oh, thank you, and God bless you!" I said as I took the paper with the address on it. "This is the happiest day of my life! Thank you again for checking for me."

I could feel the sun smile down on me as I walked quickly toward the address. *Hilde Dittman is alive and well.* The words ran over and over in my mind.

What would I say to Mother? Had her faith remained strong during the last eighteen months? It would take us weeks to get caught up on the events of our lives. I nearly exploded with anticipation and excitement as I studied the addresses along the way.

A few of the camp's survivors were mingling about now. I suspected most of them were unbelieving Jews who desperately needed to hear a message of hope. No doubt they had lost everything, for their war-weary faces reflected their dejection. All of them were desperately thin and old beyond their years. What would Mother look like?

Finally, I stood outside Mother's building. Just then a middle-aged Jewish lady came out for some morning sun and greeted me.

"I am Anita Dittman," I said to her. "Is my mother at this address?"

"Why, yes, she is!" Hennie Rosenberg replied as her face lit up. "She has told us so much about you, Anita. I feel like you and I are old friends. Come with me up the stairs."

We wound around a seemingly endless flight of stairs until we came to the top floor of the smelly, old building.

"Six of us have been sharing one tiny room since the war ended," Hennie said apologetically. "It's kind of a mess, as you can imagine."

Finally, we stood out of breath at the top of the stairs. Hennie opened the apartment door and walked in ahead of me. Then she held the door open for me, and I saw Mother sitting on the edge of her bed, wearing the pink bathrobe I'd left in the basement of the synagogue!

Mother's eyes filled with tears as we gazed at each other, both of us frozen in place. She was pale and forty pounds lighter, but her eyes had the same sparkle I remembered. Then, without speaking, we walked toward one another. Mother put her arms on my shoulders and looked at me for a long moment before we broke into tears and embraced, silently expressing our mutual thanks to God.

"An hour ago, Anita, a bus left for Breslau. I could have gone, but I felt sure you would come here even if you had to crawl."

"You got my note, then?"

"Only because I nearly starved to death the week before you sent it. When the bread arrived, it was moldy. But I was so hungry that I had to find an edible portion. I came to the note first. The remaining bread sustained me for days. Since the day I found out about your arrest, Anita, the handful of believers here at Theresienstadt have prayed for you every day: Mrs. Bott, Mrs. Czech, and others."

"Steffi Bott and Gunther Czech were in the camp with me, Mother. Did their mothers survive?"

"Yes, they are both here. But almost 90 percent of the camp died. The Russians saved the rest of us by a day, or we would have been gassed. But tell me about you, Anita."

While Mother and I sat on her tiny cot, with her five Jewish roommates listening intently, I recounted my eleven-month ordeal. Since I sensed that her roommates were unbelievers, I tried to highlight the hand of God in my life. They listened with wide eyes and rapt attention. They gasped at my ugly leg scars but rejoiced as I told them how the wounds and scars had protected me from the Russians. Only Mother could believe my tremendous endurance and persistence in getting to Theresienstadt under the circumstances.

Then I listened as they told me the horrors of Theresienstadt.

The "showers" had been almost completely constructed, and the Cyclone B gas had already been delivered when the Russians stormed the camp.

"Perhaps God provided an angel," Mother said, "in the form of a Red Cross man. Somehow he was let into the camp before the war ended. The Nazis tried to cover up the gas chambers that were being built, but he spotted them. Then he raced by car to the advancing Russians and begged them to come here immediately. The godless Russians listened to his request and came at once. Behind them came doctors and nurses to care for our sick and dying. The camp was experiencing a terrible typhoid epidemic."

"I know all about angels, Mother."

Some of the Nazis' hideous medical experiments were performed on the Theresienstadt inhabitants. It was doubtful that many of the experiments were legitimate, and some were designed only to mutilate and inflict pain. Then, on a whim, the Nazi doctor might decide to kill the victim mercifully by an injection of air into his veins. Other prisoners, not as fortunate, were clubbed to death. Still others died from the heavy labor, while more perished from starvation.

To the unbelievers, death was their only friend. To the believers, only their faith in Christ sustained them.

However, Theresienstadt housed more than just Jews, though they were the greatest number by far. Every camp had its share of "undesirables," including communists, Gypsies, Jehovah's Witnesses, the mentally defective, and the insane. And the Nazis delighted in beheading the many homosexuals sent to the various camps.

The stories of blood, tears, and terror in Theresienstadt, Dachau, Auschwitz, Buchenwald, Bergen-Belsen, Treblinka, Ravensbruck, and other camps could fill many volumes. Satan didn't overlook a single hideous method of making humanity suffer. Mrs. Rosenberg told me how the streets of Prague literally flowed with blood as the Nazis stormed in to capture their victims. While a family watched helplessly, a baby or a small child would be clubbed and murdered by Satan on the loose, in the guise of a storm trooper.

Mother had worked long hours, often scrubbing floors all night long. She had been given several other assignments in her eighteen-month stay, for the Nazis made sure each prisoner worked hard for the privilege of life. The filth, rats, lice, and fleas were the only other things of which the prisoners could be sure. Such an existence turned many prisoners into animals; they would kill a friend over a lump of sugar.

* * *

A week after I arrived at Theresienstadt, Steffi Bott's mother did locate her, and they were happily reunited.

A month later the Russians moved all of us to Bavaria, to a displaced persons camp swarming with homeless Jews from all over

Europe. For seven months Steffi and I and our mothers shared one room in the DP camp while our papers were processed and we were assigned new homes. Relatives of the Botts in New York would sponsor their trip to America.

Because of England's financial problems, we could not go there to be with Hella. Instead, the American Christian Committee for Refugees helped us go to America.

In May 1946, we left the DP camp and went by cattle car to Bremen, Germany. The roofs of the cars had sizable holes, which provided good, fresh air, until one night when it poured rain. Then our mattresses on the floor turned into "waterbeds," and our food, clothing, and luggage were drenched.

After more processing in Bremen, we went on to its port, Bremerhaven. Then on June 7, 1946, a bright, sunny day, Steffi and I and our mothers, plus nearly nine hundred other refugees, embarked on the SS *Marine Flasher*, bound for America. Mixed emotions overcame everyone that morning as the German shoreline disappeared, for the country held so many memories—both good and bad—for all of us. We stood on the deck and squinted into the sun as Germany grew faint.

For eleven days we bounced over the ocean en route to America on a journey of mingled joy, fears of the unknown, adventure, and the formation of new friendships.

On June 17, 1946, we were told that we would arrive in New York the following morning. All the young people on board stayed up all night to catch the first glimpse of America at dawn. We chattered and laughed and waited expectantly all night on the upper deck. As the first rays of sunlight peeked over the horizon, we could see the Statue of Liberty pointing up through the foggy sky. No one spoke.

An hour later, when we passed the Statue of Liberty, everyone stood speechless on deck. How fitting that the words of a Jew, poet Emma Lazarus, should be engraved on that work of art, welcoming a boatload of nine hundred homeless Jewish refugees to freedom. All of us had dreamed of tasting that freedom every day for the last thirteen years.

epiLogue

Dozens of our relatives and friends were never heard from again. We could only assume that they made up that vast, impersonal figure of six million slaughtered Jews who were dumped into massive, unmarked graves. Such must have been the fate of Aunt Käte, Aunt Friede, Aunt Elsbeth, and other relatives and friends.

But in the years to come, contact with a few would be restored. Father survived the war but died of cancer in 1974. Hella, too, passed away from cancer in 1965. I never did see my father again, although we corresponded. Even so, he rejected my attempts to witness to him, as did my sister. To my sorrow, they died atheists.

The Wolf brothers had perished toward the end of the war. Christian Risel found his parents alive and remained in Germany after the war. He became a pharmacist, and we corresponded for many years.

Gunther Czech also survived and remained in Germany.

Last, but certainly not least, Pastor Hornig and his lovely wife survived the Holocaust. Pastor Hornig was struck by a truck in 1976, while still living in Germany, and never recovered from the accident. Mrs. Hornig also died many years ago.

The wonderful believers at St. Barbara's Lutheran Church in Breslau were a few of Germany's heroes. Sadly, the number of heroes was scarce. Many pastors and churches sold out to the Nazis or else turned a deaf ear and a blind eye to the suffering of Europe's incarcerated. Satan worked himself into the very heart of the church in Germany and caused many church people—pastors and laymen alike—to rationalize and compromise with the Nazis. A hear-no-evil, see-no-evil mentality swept the country with regard to her treatment of the Jews and other "undesirables." When Germans were questioned about things they had seen, the whole nation suddenly developed a strange form of "amnesia." Perhaps it was a self-protecting device that helped them forget the terrible ordeal of Nazi Germany.

The nation that had produced Beethoven, Bach, Mozart, and a host of other men and women for whom the world will always be grateful, also perpetrated and, often actively or passively, supported the carnage of the Third Reich.

But the casualties hit home, too, for Germany was a massive, burned-out crater by the end of the war. Three million of her soldiers died, and another million shivered in the prisons of Siberia. More than half a million civilians perished in the air raids over Germany.

But what nation is not capable of the same kind of tyranny? While Germany killed her six million prisoners, Russia killed twenty million in Siberia. Later, Stalin heaped countless other lives on top of that. The bamboo curtain imprisons millions more. The same kind of treatment and torture is inflicted upon those living today in dozens of other countries.

It is clear that the spirit of Adolf Hitler is alive in the world today, for that spirit is Satan. Even as Germany believed Hitler's lies, the world believes Satan's lies, for he is the father of lies. Ironically Hitler himself was deceived, saving his most savage attacks for the unarmed Jews rather than for the armies that destroyed him. Even in his final words he denounced the threat of international Jewry.

That same spirit fans the flames of anti-Semitism today. While

Russian Jews are less persecuted since the fall of Communism, a Jew is risking his or her life on the streets of many European nations. Some say that the anti-Semitic climate in Europe today nearly rivals that of 1939. The Jews of Europe are fleeing to Israel in fear. In the UK, anti-Semitic attacks have increased 42 percent since 2004.

Evil in the name of God exists in many of today's Christian denominations. The Presbyterian Church (U.S.A.), Methodist Church, Episcopal Church USA, and the World and National Councils of Churches have all voted to *divest* funds in Israel, strangling her economy. And with the push for a Palestinian state, Bible prophecy is further fulfilled in that all nations are coming against Israel—perhaps even America—as prophesied in Zechariah 12:3. And as bizarre as it is, we have people like Iran's former president Mahmoud Ahmadinejad, and others, saying there never was a Holocaust while they plan a second one. Holocaust denial is on fast-forward in recent years.

Anti-Semitism takes on strange features, but the bottom line is that the Jewish people are still cursed by many people, denominations, and nations, even if they do not wear swastikas.

However, the greatest news of all is that God is ready and willing to forgive even an Adolf Hitler, an Eichmann, a Himmler, a Heydrich, a Goebbels, or a Höss. God's love and forgiveness are that great. God can transform the most wicked individual if he but acknowledges his need of the one Savior, Jesus Christ!

But if the incredibly evil do not respond to God, if they align themselves with the Evil One—God's people do not need to fear. God delivers. And if He does not deliver, He sustains. And if He does not sustain, He receives us into His everlasting arms—for He is sovereign! God be praised.

Anita, shortly after she arrived in America

photo credits

Photos on pages 28, 33, 43, 45, 113, 114, 124, 179 used by permission from the United States Holocaust Memorial Museum. "The views or opinions expressed in this book, and the context in which the images are used, do not necessarily reflect the views or policy of, nor imply approval or endorsement by, the United States Holocaust Memorial Museum."

The following images taken from BigStockPhotos; used with permission: Photo on page 53 © Marlin Thorman. Photo on page 136 © Tina Rencelj. Photo on page 149 © Patrick Tuohy. Photo on page 159 © Catherine Tranent. Photo on page 176 © Rejean Giroux. Photo on page 191 © Kent Christopherson. Photo on page 200 © Tanya Weliky. Used with permission.

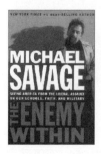
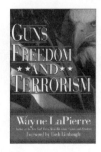
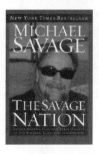

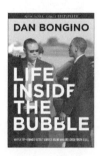
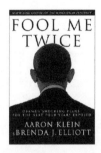

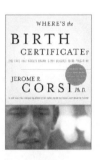

WND Books

PRESENTS

DAVID KUPELIAN

THE MARKETING OF EVIL

How Radicals,
Elitists, and Pseudo-Experts
Sell Us Corruption
Disguised as Freedom

"David Kupelian dares to tell the truth about the overwhelming forces in our society which take us away from our original American concept of freedom."
—Dr. Laura Schlessinger

The Marketing of Evil reveals how much of what Americans once almost universally abhorred has been packaged, perfumed, gift-wrapped and sold to them as though it had great value. Highly skilled marketers, playing on our deeply felt national values of fairness, generosity and tolerance, have persuaded us to embrace as enlightened and noble that which all previous generations since America's founding regarded as grossly self-destructive-in a word, evil.

WND Books · A WND COMPANY · WASHINGTON DC · WNDBOOKS.COM

 WND Books

PRESENTS

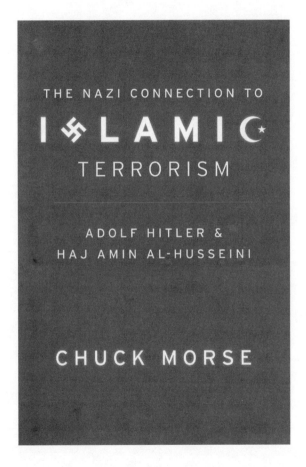

THE NAZI CONNECTION TO

I✷LAMIC☾

TERRORISM

ADOLF HITLER &
HAJ AMIN AL-HUSSEINI

CHUCK MORSE

This is the remarkable story of Haj Amin al-Husseini who was, in many ways, as big a Nazi villain as Hitler himself. To understand his influence on the Middle East is to understand the ongoing genocidal program against the Jews of Israel. Al-Husseini was a bridge figure in terms of transporting the Nazi genocide in Europe into the post-war Middle East. As the leader of Arab Palestine during the British Mandate period, al-Husseini introduced violence against moderate Arabs as well as against Jews.

WND Books • A WND COMPANY • WASHINGTON DC • WNDBOOKS.COM